Access the
right people,
Strengthen client
relationships,
and double
your sales.

SUPERNETWORKING
FOR SALES PROS

MICHAEL SALMON

CAREER
PRESS
FRANKLIN LAKES, NJ

SUPERNETWORKING FOR SALES PROS
EDITED BY JODI BRANDON
Cover design by Cheryl Cohan Finbow
Printed in the U.S.A. by Book-mart Press

To order this title, please call toll-free 1-800-CAREER-1 (NJ and Canada: 201-848-0310) to order using VISA or MasterCard, or for further information on books from Career Press.

The Career Press, Inc., 3 Tice Road, PO Box 687,
Franklin Lakes, NJ 07417
www.careerpress.com

Library of Congress Cataloging-in-Publication Data
Salmon, Michael, 1956-
    SuperNetworking for sales pros : access the right people, strengthen
    client relationships, and double your sales / by Michael Salmon.
        p. cm.
    Includes index.
    ISBN 1-56414-794-0 (pbk.)
    1. Selling. 2. Business networks. 3. Social networks. 4. Sales personnel. I Title: Supernetworking for sales pros. II. Title.

HF5438.25.S255 2005
658.85--dc22   2004063218

Dedication

To Bruce.
There is not a day that goes by
that I don't think about you.
I love you and miss you very much.

Acknowledgments

Carl Baskind, you are a saint. Again, your insight, candor, intuition, and contribution were exactly what I needed. I am eternally grateful. Thank you for being there for me.

Doug Rothman, Alice O'Neil, Karl Wagner, Cathy Burgess, Dan Alletag, David Gomes, and Tom Ryder, your voices were heard loud and clear. Thank you for your time, comments, suggestions, and objectivity.

Lou Lanzillo, just another chapter in our story. Thank you for suggesting that this subject matter become my second book.

Gerry Sindell, your insights are always on the mark. Thank you for your help crystallizing and positioning concepts reflected in the book.

Michael Snell, we are now two-for-two. Your counsel, guidance, and convictions resulted in the publication of my second book. Thank you again for believing in me and my vision.

My beautiful wife Holly, I love you and appreciate you more than you know. I value and treasure those feelings every day. Thank you for your love, support, confidence, conviction, and tolerance.

My daughter Alex, the real author in the family. It was a great thrill working with you side by side. I hope this experience becomes Bailey's launching pad. Thank you for helping me.

To my other children, Evan and Adrienne, everything I do is for all three of you. Thank you for your continued support and inspiring talks.

Contents

Foreword

How Was
SuperNetworking
Developed?

My background is 25-plus years of sales as well as marketing and general management positions for both privately held and publicly traded companies. Early on in my career I became the consistent #1 sales representative out of 120 people for a Fortune 500 company. I began to notice that what I was doing was different from most of the other 119 sales people. I realized that I was consistently asking my clients for help in introducing me to people they knew. Referrals were vastly better than cold calling. That was the beginning.

Over time I began to shift my networking efforts from casual to intentional. Now I didn't just ask for referrals from happy customers. Instead, I began to develop target customers, and then build my network directed toward that targeted customer, link by link. I was asking clients and contacts for referrals based on specific criteria I used to describe the type of business I was targeting. I made it easy for my contacts to give me referrals of not just names, but people who knew the "right people"—and sometimes the "right people" themselves. I found that I was getting my voice heard and closed a lot of business. I didn't quite realize it at the time, but I was not just networking to get more business: I was *SuperNetworking*.

As I had a chance to reflect on my professional experience I realized that the key ingredients to my success were developing excellent customer relationships and asking my clients for help in introducing me to people they know. I have not made a cold call in many years. Some of my current clients are Merrill Lynch, Smith Barney, Evergreen Investments, Fidelity Capital, Federated Investors, United Technologies, and New York Life. What's important here is not the companies but the people in those companies with whom I was able to develop solid relationships. It just so happens that they work for well-recognized firms. It is these people who have opened up additional doors for me to create an invaluable network of contacts for life. I am now managing more than 150 additional new client relationships in various stages of development, and all of these opportunities have come from referrals.

I realized, early on, that the rapport I established with my contacts and referrals was merely a door-opener. All it did was give me an opportunity to get my voice heard. I knew that I would earn my credibility by the way I conducted myself during my initial call to my target. I found that, if all things are equal relative to price, product, and service, chances are that if I arrived by way of my network I was going to get the sale. Time and again I realized that my network gave me a genuine competitive advantage. The ageless expression "it's not what you know, but whom you know" illustrates the power of human beings' enormous need to trust. If you come to me as a friend of my friend,

I am inclined to initially trust you more than a perfect stranger and give you preferential treatment. Is this fair? Maybe not, but that's the way human beings function.

No other sales training methodology shows people how to build on your existing network of contacts and develop those into your own *SuperNetwork*. You will find that this book was written in a positive, easy-to-follow, matter-of-fact style that will make it simple for you to develop, incorporate, and implement a plan to go after new business opportunities. This book will give you a systematic approach and show you how to become engaged in the sales process, get you in front of the right person, radically increase your business volume, increase the quality of the business you do, and make more money for you and your organization now and in the long term. *SuperNetworking for Sales Pros* will become your golden parachute forever.

Introduction

6 Degrees of Separation

The Landscape of Selling Has Changed

Getting access to decision-makers is not as easy as it used to be. Buyers have become slower when making decisions and are not buying as much as they used to. In some instances, they are reluctant to give you your asking price, fearing their boss will second-guess them or that they need to show they negotiated a discount. Buyers are also afraid of saying "yes" too quickly, thinking if they wait they may get a better deal. Does this sound familiar?

In this tough economic climate, generating revenue is a big challenge. Many people in an organization can have an effect on whether a sale will go through or not. That is why knowing how to infiltrate an organization and access the right person (or people) will give sales professionals a competitive advantage. Leveraging a network of contacts to get more business may appear to be an obvious notion, but only a small percentage (less than 20 percent of all salespeople) network effectively. Most successful salespeople will tell you they never cold call. They will also tell you they spend most of their time with current clients, and they get most of their new business contacts and actual new business from leveraging the existing relationships they have.

According to *Sales & Marketing Management* magazine "warm calls" have a 90-percent response rate, and "cold calls" have a less-than-10-percent rate of response. Referrals will help you open doors you could not open on your own. Every now and then we need to be reminded that the expression "it's not what you know, but whom you know" is true. Referrals and contacts will help open doors you may not be able to.

If Referrals Are so Terrific, Why Don't Most People Ask Their Clients or People They Know for Referrals?

For people who are either uncomfortable asking or have never been shown a system, this is a "how to" for building and using a network. *SuperNetworking* will be your guide so you are not cold calling for every new account and will open doors you couldn't open on your own.

SuperNetworking is the first method that transforms the concept of networking from being something vague and arbitrary into a sustainable system that is swift, deliberate, effective, and easy to follow. *SuperNetworking* is a system that will consistently get you access to the people you want to speak to, in front of the right person, and also assure that those right people are willing to hear what you have to say.

SuperNetworking provides a methodical approach for identifying a specific target for a specific reason and then figuring out the best links to get there. With goals clearly in mind, *SuperNetworking* will show you how to expand your base of business contacts, leverage your existing relationships, extract promises from your contacts, attain the outcome you desire, provide an effective way to track progress and results, and measure your return on investment (ROI).

You can go to college and get a degree in marketing, computer science, accounting, or finance, but not sales. It has been said that sales is something you either understand instinctively or something you develop through some form of sales training. Other sales training books and programs will offer lots of value once you are engaged in the process and speaking to the right person. However, if you are not engaged or can't access the right person to get your voice heard, you can't sell your product or service, and all of the other sales skills you develop are worthless.

That means this skill, *SuperNetworking*, is foundational. You need to learn *SuperNetworking* before you can begin to employ your other sales training skills. Referrals are a way to create a life in which you're only making warm calls and opening doors that you couldn't on your own. No other sales training methodology shows you how to build on your own existing network of contacts and develop into your own *SuperNetwork*. If you constantly invest in your network, you will find that your Rolodex will have high value content and give you the long-term financial and job security that earlier generations gained from working with just one company.

Taking Control of Your Destination: How *SuperNetworking* Can Help

SuperNetworking will provide you with a complete, simple, practical, easy-to-follow, methodical, proactive approach to access current and future contacts and clients and will show you how to take an empowered approach to your business. You must drive your business by holding people accountable to their commitments. How many times have people said they were going to do things for you, such as make a phone call or set up a meeting on your behalf, and it never happens?

The program will work for you, provided you are willing to do the work. There are no shortcuts to success. It is hard work, but the payoff is worth it. Here is just a quick example of what I am talking about.

> *One of my target vertical markets is the financial services sector. Recently, I targeted a specific company with which I wanted to work. I called a friend of mine, Ted, who is a senior vice president of one of the nation's largest mutual fund companies, headquartered in Boston. I told him about my work with other financial service companies and stated that I thought I could help his company, too. I asked if he could help me access the right person in the company to whom I should speak. He placed a call on my behalf and cleared the way for me to call Patricia. I called Patricia and she put me in touch with one of her key people, Maura. I called Maura, and we had a great conversation. I was able to articulate my understanding of her industry, organization, and current challenges. After a few meetings we were able to scope out a program for their business unit. The company is now a client.*

Without making those deliberate steps to build those specific connections, painting that clear mental picture to Ted of exactly what I was looking for, and making it easy for him to help, I never would have been able to access the right person. It is highly unlikely that this particular organization would ever have discovered us as a resource. The difference is in recognizing and utilizing the power of *SuperNetworking*.

This kind of *SuperNetworking* was a true win-win-win situation. I picked up more business, our workshops contributed to Ted's company's sales growth in 2004, and Ted's status as a "well-connected person" was enhanced. That's part of the power of *SuperNetworking (specific target, specific reason, and best links to get there)*. This book will show you how to access and get in front of the right person more frequently. This methodology gets you into the batter's box on a consistent basis so you are spending most of your time swinging for the fences. *SuperNetworking* will take you there.

To get the best results you must have a plan, a process to follow. As former Treasury Secretary Paul O'Neil said, "Great process gives you great results." If you want to exceed expectations and make more money, you will implement what you read in this book. If you don't want to make more money, go on "warm" calls, have a lot more activity with more qualified prospects, exceed quota, or have more time for leisure activities, then stop reading right here and continue to do things the way you were doing them before. But if you really do want to have more personal and professional success and make more money, you have to be ready to change your thought process and approach.

This book will provide you with that process, step by step. You will learn *what* to do, but more importantly you'll be shown *how* to do it. By the end of the book, you will have developed the necessary ingredients and gained the know-how to:

◆ **Prospect** to get better referrals and introductions and improve the quality of your clients.

- ◆ **Cultivate** relationships that will provide a steady flow of referrals.
- ◆ **Increase** your book of business every year.

In Chapter 1, you are going to learn the value of being organized and work on a self-analysis, your professional analysis, and your elevator pitch. The self-analysis will help you clarify your core competency and your personal and professional characteristics. The answers to these questions will help you crystallize your value proposition in a way that will make it easy for others to buy from you or help you network with the right people. Also, you will learn how to develop an effective "elevator pitch" and be shown how to create specific pitches for a variety of business and social situations. You will learn how to capture your target audience's attention within 30 seconds and how to articulate what that person needs to know in order to help you grow your business.

In Chapter 2, you will learn how not to spin your wheels, but rather how to create an effective road map to ensure you have a sound strategy and reach your objective for every call you make. This chapter will give you a plan and all the tools you need to make a strong impression on each contact and referral. You will learn how to make it easy for these people to help you so that it will not feel like an inconvenience or a hardship. You will be able to articulate and demonstrate your value proposition so well that contacts and referrals will feel very comfortable and motivated to help you.

In Chapter 3, you will learn how to qualify personal and professional contacts by order of importance and categorize them appropriately. You will also learn how to "peel the onion" and how to use those contacts to find more contacts, thus increasing the number of people on your list and the warm calls you will make. In essence you will learn how to go through numerous layers of contacts and referrals until you get to the core—the right person who can and will help you. You will learn the distinction between a "contact" and a "referral" and the importance of knowing how to manage each relationship. You will also learn why using someone's name to open a door does not guarantee a successful call or his or her business, the importance of being credible, and the three types of credibility you have when making calls to referrals.

In Chapter 4, you are going to realize the value of making a favorable impression by preparing for all of your conversations. You will learn how to gather critical information about individuals and companies and where to get it. You will also review a series of questions that will provide great insight and help you discover your potential value to your targeted individual or company. Most salespeople feel they can just wing it, because it has been working for them in the past, and hope for the best. They generally fail. You are going to get one shot to make a strong impression with your contacts; successful preparation for the call will bring you closer to a new account.

In Chapter 5, you will learn the essential things you need to do in every contact moment, whether on the phone or in person. You will be given a thorough guide of the key networking do's and don'ts, learn how to tactfully use someone else's name, and manage this stage of the networking process in order to open doors to help you always make a favorable impression.

In Chapter 6, you will learn how to create and use a call script, which will be developed from the work you did in prior chapters, formulating your self-analysis, elevator pitch, due diligence, strategy, and call objective. Sample time-tested scripts and techniques will be provided to help you prepare your own.

You will be shown the distinction between contact, client, and referral calls, how to approach each of these people as part of your network, and what to say to get the outcome you desire. You will review a step-by-step, chronological order of the critical elements that make a successful script. You will also be given effective, time-tested techniques and sample scripts that will disarm the toughest gatekeepers (the people who get paid to keep you from gaining access to the decision-maker), and you'll learn about voice mails that get people to call back and how to handle situations when someone gives you the "cold shoulder."

In Chapter 7, you will learn how to build, maintain, and use a network database for keeping track of your contacts for selling and maintaining a network for life. You will learn the importance of being able to readily access information by fields, how to use the database to keep the sales process moving forward, and how to track progress. In addition, you will learn when and how often to stay in touch with different people in your database to keep your network strong.

In Chapter 8, you will learn why this plan will not work if you don't report your progress to someone. Everyone needs a boss to report to when you are responsible for driving revenue for an organization, whether you are an owner, manager, sole practitioner, or salesperson. In order for you to succeed in implementing this networking program you must have a mentor who will help formalize the process, monitor your progress, ensure that you stay focused, and improve your productivity.

After you launch your *SuperNetworking* plan you will become so busy with making phone calls, sending e-mails, scheduling meetings, going on more sales calls, submitting more proposals, and following up that you could easily lose focus and effectiveness. You don't want things "slipping through the cracks." Most plans, such as diets, fail because, even though you start out with good intentions, you become distracted and start to rationalize why you stopped. You don't want to be the salesperson who starts out having success and then starts taking shortcuts and has poor or inconsistent follow-up and follow-through. This is something for which most unsuccessful salespeople get criticized.

You will learn how to select the best person to be your mentor and why you need to meet with him or her on a weekly basis. You will also learn the values of having this person keep you on track and provide valuable support, as well as how he or she will help you improve your efficiency and effectiveness.

In Chapter 9, you will learn that, in order for this process to work, ensuring that you and your company receive a favorable return on your investment, you need to incorporate an accountability mechanism. You will be given a sample progress report with set standards for unacceptable, acceptable, and exceptional standards of performance, providing a reality check on where you are relative to your goals and objectives, and the critical success factors that are essential to your success. This progress report will become the framework for the weekly discussions you have with your boss or mentor.

By Chapter 10, you will learn that making more money and generating more sales was just the byproduct of the work you did and the new skill you developed: the art of *SuperNetworking*.

You will take a long look forward and learn the importance of constantly updating your contact list and keeping it fresh. You will learn why this is just the beginning of a lifelong process of *SuperNetworking*. You will learn what you have to do to treat your network as you would a treasure, which needs to be nourished, preserved, and developed.

You will learn the power and value of having a *SuperNetwork* not just for business but for other purposes, too, such as getting tickets to a ball game, finding a great restaurant, or helping someone get into an exclusive club. By doing this, the next time you are in a position of needing help, whether it is to expand your business or find the best place in town to get your hair cut, you will not have to look so far or work so hard to make things happen.

You will also learn that networking is a two-way street of giving and receiving. At the beginning of this process you were the beneficiary of help from others, whether it was opening doors, making introductions, or helping you close an account. You will now be in a position to return the favor, help others, and give something back. That's part of the deal. It's an unwritten understanding that you will help others. You are now going to be the person giving advice or allowing others to use your name to open up a door. That's part of the responsibility of being a *SuperNetworker*: giving back and staying in touch, not just when you need a favor.

Let's Get Started

SuperNetworking for Sales Pros is for everybody. For the new or junior salesperson this book will provide you with a system that will help you start building a network of contacts. For mid-level and senior people, you will learn a highly refined methodology that will reinforce some of the basic concepts you knew about networking and get you selling to your highest potential. For large sales organizations, *SuperNetworking* can transform the sales process so that salespeople from top to bottom start to consistently get more quality appointments that will lead to better business. Small to medium-sized business organizations that do not have a sales manager and need to incorporate a system to generate more revenue will now be given a methodology to follow to leverage their existing relationships in a manner that fits with their personalities. For everyone, *SuperNetworking* is about working smarter, not harder. Your next sales opportunity is right there for you; it is in your *SuperNetwork*.

By the time you are finished reading this book, here is what you will have learned. In the end a *SuperNetworker* will:

- ✦ Better understand your personal and professional strengths, company, and competitive advantages.
- ✦ Articulate your value proposition and talents to your target audience in a short, effective pitch.
- ✦ Conduct research and due diligence to target the right people.
- ✦ Avoid the big no-no's of networking.
- ✦ Meet more people to maximize new opportunities.
- ✦ Improve the volume and quality of your book of business.
- ✦ Be more comfortable in any setting.
- ✦ Build and maintain your network for life.
- ✦ Become a well-connected person.
- ✦ Generate more revenue for your business.
- ✦ Make more money for yourself.

This book offers a systematic approach to opening more doors, leveraging existing contacts, and delivering a time-tested process that will immediately improve your sales results. The stories used in this book are true. The names and companies were changed to preserve their anonymity.

Chapter 1

Get Introspective:

Quantify and Articulate Your Strengths

Typically most salespeople are recreating the wheel every day. They are cold-calling most of the time; they rarely receive incoming referral calls, and they can't access the decision-maker or speak to the right person. Most successful salespeople will tell you they never "cold-call." They will also tell you they spend most of their time with current clients and they get most of their new business contacts and actual new business from leveraging existing relationships they have. Do you ever wonder why they are so comfortable leveraging relationships for new business?

In his regional sales force of 50 people, Rob was used to always being at the top. He prided himself on his ability to be an excellent communicator, a people person, a guy who could think on his feet, "wing it," and get results he needed.

Doesn't that describe most salespeople?

But now Rob realized that the market was chang-ing and his old strategy was just not working like it used to. He was not getting referrals anymore, and he was making way too many cold calls. He decided to get introspective in order to turn things around. He started working on a turnaround plan by implement-ing the concepts he learned from the SuperNetworking *program. He began by conducting an analysis of his personal and professional strengths and getting clear on what distinguished his and his company's offerings from the competition's offerings. He began to clearly communicate what he discovered, both when calling clients and when asking for referrals. The results were immediate. In the first 11 months of sticking to his new* SuperNetworking *process, Rob had exceeded his quota and was so busy with prospect meetings, making pre-sentations, preparing and submitting proposals, and having numerous follow-up meetings that he didn't need to make cold calls.*

You are thinking, *this is too good to be true*, right? Sec-ondly, you are starting to think of calling people you know to get more and better qualified leads. You know that makes perfect sense but you are not quite sure of the best way to approach them.

As Rob did, whether you are an expert or novice at networking, you need to have a plan that gives you focus, purpose, strategy, and tactics. You also need it to mea-sure your progress and results. The first two things you need to do are to learn how to:

1. Determine the value you bring to an organization or an individual.
2. Articulate your value proposition to your specific target audience.

Self-Analysis

The first step in your journey is getting to know yourself, your company, your service offerings, and your competition. You need to be clear about what makes you successful both personally and professionally, and also determine what differentiates you and your company's service offering from the competition. To do this you must quantify your personal and professional strengths and learn how to clearly articulate your talents and the benefits of your service.

Knowing yourself and your company and being able to communicate clearly who you are, are core competencies that will prepare you for future conversations and meetings with contacts and referrals, where you will be able to demonstrate your "value proposition." Being able to clearly articulate your strengths, as well as your company's strengths, and communicate exactly what you can deliver will separate you from your competition. Your competition generally lacks focus and will probably be "winging it."

As you begin *SuperNetworking*, be confident that this journey will get you to your destination. It's important that you enjoy the journey, because you are going to find opportunities along the way, possibly in places you hadn't imagined, such as at your child's soccer game or on an airplane. As one door you thought would be open closes, another one will present itself to you. You need to be ready to walk right through it. You are about to develop new relationships that will help you, and, as of now, you don't really know where many of those relationships will be coming from. That's life. Life is what happens in between your plans. You never know when that magic moment will occur when you meet someone who could open a door for you or become your new or biggest account. So be ready.

You need to get ready to put pen to paper and complete a self-analysis. The answers to these questions will become your personal profile to which you will often refer back in subsequent chapters. Completing the self-analysis will help you clarify what it is that you want people to know about you, clarify your company's service offering, and help you create a clear mental picture based on specific criteria to describe types of business you are targeting.

Use these examples as a reference as you complete your own self-analysis. Meet Alex and Gail. Alex is an experienced financial advisor for a financial services company, and Gail is junior salesperson for a chemical cleaning supply company.

Self-Analysis #1:
Alex, experienced financial advisor

Part I

What is my area of expertise? Sales and marketing in the financial service sector. Driving revenue and profits.

What has made me successful? I am always well prepared, have good listening skills, respond to customer hot buttons, am reliable, and have strong follow-through. Besides focusing on the professional needs of the customers and their organizations, I am sensitive to the customer's personal needs and interests.

What should people know about me personally? I am passionate, hardworking, dedicated, loyal, committed, honest, and very direct. I enjoy sharing knowledge with others and spending time on my boat. My family is very important to me. In addition, I have always been involved in team and individual sports.

What should people know about me professionally? I am results-oriented. I deliver what I promise. I have demonstrated a track record of increasing revenue and profitability in every organization I have worked for. I stay abreast of industry trends and consistently introduce breakthrough products to clients.

What distinguishes me from my competition? I am knowledgeable, dedicated, hardworking, passionate, proactive, honest, and reliable. I know what needs to be done and I execute. I am well versed in all aspects of business. I produce above-average returns to my clients annually.

Part II

What can customers accomplish from working with me and my company? (features) A thorough process to assess their situation and come up with a customized plan to reach their financial goals. Innovative products, access to industry experts, one-stop shop for a full range of financial service needs and service, consistent and reliable returns, the best products, sound advice, trust, and loyalty.

What are the benefits of developing a relationship with my company and me? Peace of mind, confidence that we are the best company for them, real value added from the depth of our expertise to the many areas of service that we can offer, whether they need business loans or want us to manage their entire portfolio.

What should potential customers know about my service delivery? (tie in features and benefits) A thorough process to assess their situations and come up with customized plans to reach their financial goals gives our clients a high degree of confidence in our ability to do the right thing for them. Our innovative products are cutting edge, and no one else in our industry can offer better programs.

Having access to industry experts lets our clients know that we are resourceful and we can help them in any aspect of their financial planning needs with a one-stop shop for a full range of financial service offerings. Our consistent and reliable returns every year ensure that our clients can rely on their portfolios increasing at greater rates. By offering the best products and sound advice, clients come to know that I am client-focused, which gives them peace of mind. The trust and loyalty gained from my clients has resulted in positive and lasting professional and personal relationships.

What differentiates my service from my competition? Our service delivery model, innovative products, thorough time-tested consultative process, our access to expertise, full range of service offerings, commitment to client satisfaction, and all of our employees are shareholders.

Why should a potential customer work with me and not my competition? I am knowledgeable, dedicated, hard-working, passionate, proactive, honest, and reliable. I know what needs to be done and I execute.

Our thorough process to assess their situation allows us to customize a plan to reach their financial goals, and it's second to none. Our innovative products are cutting edge, and no one else in our industry can offer better programs. Our depth of service offerings gives them access to industry experts they can't find elsewhere who can help them in any aspect of their financial planning. Our consistent and reliable returns every year guarantee an above-industry return for them every year.

I am client-focused and take a proactive approach by reviewing and rebalancing if necessary. This type of approach will give them peace of mind that I am looking out for their best interests 24/7.

How can I create or demonstrate the value my service delivers? Provide statistical data to back up every feature and benefit mentioned and marketing materials on every product we offer. Extend an offer to come to our client offices and meet our industry experts and the management team so they can see the knowledge, depth, and professionalism of our organization. Lastly, potential clients can speak to some of my other clients that have similar interests and expectations.

♦ ♦ ♦

Self Analysis #2:
Gail, junior salesperson

Part I

What is my area of expertise? My ability to identify the best products and machinery to get the job done effectively and improve efficiencies for my clients.

What has made me successful? My hard work, likeable personality, technical skills, ability to influence others, and customer service skills.

What should people know about me personally? I am honest, loyal, reliable, and humble, and I have a good sense of humor.

What should people know about me professionally? Excellent follow-through, good listener, being proactive, and being resourceful.

What distinguishes me from my competition? My service delivery, customer service skills, and response.

Part II

What can a customer accomplish from working with me and my company? (features) They get consistent delivery of service from a company with more than 50 years of experience that is knowledgeable in servicing real estate clients all over the United States.

What are the benefits of developing a relationship with my company and me? A clean facility every day keeps the customer happy. With our size and levels of expertise in particular areas, we have the resources locally and nationally to solve any facilities-related problem. With this one-stop approach they don't have to look elsewhere for any of their maintenance supply needs.

What should potential customers know about my service delivery? (tie in features and benefits) We remain vigilant in being proactive to keep the customer happy. Also, we are cost competitive and provide value-added service, not just material, but with a knowledgeable service team. Our expertise along with a "do whatever it takes" attitude to deliver the best and most cost-effective materials keeps our customers' property always looking great.

What differentiates my service from the competition? Our seasoned, well-trained, and knowledgeable management team and the stability and years of service of our workforce and managers. Our people are the difference. We consistently promote from within. The level of and the amount of training people receive ensure efficiency, consistency, and service delivery second to none.

Why should a potential customer buy from me and not my competition? They can count me on 24/7. When they buy from us, even though we are big, I am going to own their accounts. They are mine. I love taking over an account and making a big difference. I know the business.

I know real estate. I know the demands. I am knowledgeable and there to support the account.

How can I create or demonstrate the value my product delivers? Reference accounts.

Take them to the accounts and have them talk directly to the clients.

◆ ◆ ◆

Now that you have read a couple samples, take a few minutes and complete your own self-analysis.

Self-Analysis

Part I

(WRITE YOUR ANSWERS BELOW.)

What is my area of expertise?

_____

_____

What has made me successful?

_____

_____

What should people know about me personally?

_____

_____

What should people know about me professionally?

_____

_____

What distinguishes me from my competition?

_____

_____

Part II

Now that you have a good idea about your field of knowledge, you must answer some questions about the benefits of doing business with you and your company.

What can a customer accomplish from working with me and my company? (features)

_____

_____

What are the benefits of developing a relationship with my company and me?

_____

_____

What should potential customers know about my service delivery? (tie in features and benefits)

_____

_____

What differentiates my service from my competition?

_____

_____

Why should a potential customer work with me and not my competition?

_____

_____

How can I create or demonstrate the value my service delivers?

_____

_____

◆ ◆ ◆

Developing your self-analysis helped you gain a better understanding of your personal and professional strengths. Your answers have helped you crystallize your value proposition in a way that will make it easy for others to buy from you or help you network to the right person. Now we want to work on getting someone interested in what you have to say and having him help you.

Have you ever spoken to someone who sounded so canned, robotic, or boring that it seemed it really didn't matter whether you were there or not? Have you ever held the phone away from your ear because the person on the other line was rambling, and when you came back to the phone the person was still rambling? Or someone is talking to you in person and you start to "zone out" because he is boring you to tears? Obviously these people had no idea you were turned off and were not paying attention because they kept on talking. Maybe you have done that to someone? Just kidding! That's why we are going to work on your articulation, or elevator pitch, to make sure you do not become this person.

You are going to develop an elevator pitch where you will apply what you have learned about yourself in your self-analysis. If you haven't completed your self-analysis already, you must do so because you need that information to prepare your elevator pitch.

Elevator Pitch

The concept of an elevator pitch is simple. If you are on an elevator with an individual with whom you want to speak, you have 30 seconds to make a favorable and lasting impression. The elevator pitch is designed to capture your target audience's interest and attention. You've either got them or lost them in that time period.

When you meet someone for the first time you will obviously take a few minutes with some pleasantries or questions, a "warm up." Eventually there will come the time when the opportunity presents itself where you talk about yourself personally or professionally. That is when you deliver your elevator pitch. Remember what Gordon Gecko said to Bud Fox in the movie *Wall Street*? "Life boils down to a few moments." When you get your chance, you must be ready!

This pitch is used in many situations: on the phone talking to contacts and referrals; meeting people at a dry cleaner; running into someone on the bus or at a luncheon, wedding, conference, trade show, or dinner party; or virtually any other social or business-type setting. Your pitch may vary depending on the type of venue or circumstances.

You need to make sure your pitch is focused, not broad. Use what you have compiled about yourself in the self-analysis and incorporate what you think are the key thing(s) you want to articulate. The elements of an effective pitch incorporate:

- ♦ **Clearly articulating who you are and what you want your target audience to know about you.**
- ♦ **What distinguishes you and/or your company.**
- ♦ **Having an objective (that is, what do you want to accomplish during this conversation?).**

Here are a few sample pitches that will help you prepare your own. In some situations you find yourself strictly talking business, in others it's strictly pleasure, and then sometimes you are mixing both. It's a fine line, and you can't afford to overstep your boundaries in any type of scenario. The scripts you will read will serve more as a guideline than a rule. After looking at these scripts, you need to create a few "elevator pitches" that make sense to you and with which that you feel comfortable. You need to incorporate your personality to create an elevator pitch so that you will come across as believable and credible to your target audience. I urge you to practice it until you get comfortable with it and it comes off naturally. Remember: You never get a second chance to make a first impression.

Situation 1: Wedding

Stan, a sales representative for Tellcomm Business Solutions, a company that offers full-service business communication solutions, is at his cousin's wedding. Here are two types of approaches he can use when talking about himself professionally and personally.

Option A

"I am Stan Collins. I am sales rep for Telcomm Business Solutions. We provide best-in-class integrated solutions for business communications, offering a single point of contact for your local, long distance, and Internet services. Our sweet spot is medium- to large-sized companies in Rhode Island with more than 150 employees. What's your line of work?"

In this scenario Stan provided a lot of information and covered the three critical elements of an elevator pitch. You know who he is and what he does. Stan used the phrases *"best-in-class"* and *"our sweet spot is medium- to large-sized companies in Rhode Island with more than 150 employees"* to distinguish his company's competitive advantages. What Stan also did was create a mental picture of his profile of companies he targets. Lastly, Stan tied in his objective by asking the probing question, *"What's your line of work?"* It was simple, easy to follow, and very focused.

Option B

"I am Stan Collins. I am Frank's first cousin. I live in town over on Chestnut Street. This is my wife, Shelly. We've got three kids ages 17, 15, and 11, and my greatest joy is spending time with them. Are you married? Do you have any children?"

In this scenario, Stan gave his target audience a nice picture of who he is personally. Then, he asked a question that could lead to additional dialogue. Even though Stan did not talk about himself professionally, he still had all the key elements in his pitch. He told the target audience something about himself that he wanted to get across, it was easy to follow, and he had an objective: to find out about his target audience by taking a personal approach.

Situation 2: Business-After-Hours Function

Hope, a sales representative for DCDS, one of the nation's largest health benefit providers, is attending a chamber of commerce business-after-hours function.

Option A

"Hi. I am Hope Busey. I have been with DCDS for 10 years in sales. We are one of the country's largest health benefit providers. Some of my clients are corporate headquarters and university and hospital employees. We are known for our outstanding customer service, quality of products, and size of our network providers. I am here tonight to make at least five new contacts with organizations that would have a need for our services. What brings you here tonight?"

What do you think? It was clear, concise, and easy to understand. You knew exactly what Hope does and what her profile of target accounts is. She made it easy for her target audience to think about whom they may know at the function, and perhaps they could possibly introduce them to Hope. Some of you may be thinking that Hope was too specific and could turn off her target audience by stating she wanted to make at least five contacts as her objective. Let's not forget the situation: It is a chamber of commerce function. Generally, people at these events are looking for more business. They do not sugarcoat it, although some of you may have been to business or networking events where people have done so. So let's give Hope some credit here for being up-front and crystal clear about her objective.

Option B

"Hi. I am Hope Busey. I have been with DCDS for 10 years in sales. We are one of the country's top health benefit

providers. Some of my clients are corporate headquarters and university and hospital employees. We are known for our outstanding customer service, quality of products, and size of our network providers. I am here tonight to make new contacts. What do you do for Main Street Bank?"

In this scenario Hope tempered it a little bit. She does not mention a specific number of new leads she wants but still makes her position clear. She covered the three key ingredients for an effective elevator pitch. With this type of approach she has given herself a subtle probing question to cover her objective and also an opportunity to engage in a more lengthy dialogue to see if they can find common ground and perhaps get a few referrals.

Situation 3: Golf Outing

Jack Landry, a financial advisor for Burell Finch, one of the world's leading financial services firms, is playing in a golf outing. Jack sees a prospective client that he's been trying to get on the phone on the putting green before the event begins.

Option A

"Hi Harvey, I am Jack Landry with Burrell Finch. I realize you are about to tee off in a few minutes. I just wanted to say hello. My expertise is helping successful business owners like you to grow assets, maximize financial security, and give the minimum to Uncle Sam. I have followed your company's growth and success and have tremendous respect for what you have accomplished in a short period of time. I was wondering if I could get your card and perhaps we can speak at greater length next Tuesday afternoon."

Option B

"Hi Harvey, I am Jack Landry with Burrell Finch. I realize you are about to tee off in a few minutes. I just wanted to say hello. Do you have a minute?

"I have followed your company's growth and success, and have tremendous respect for what you have accomplished in a short period of time. My expertise is helping successful business owners such as yourself to grow assets, maximize financial security, and give the minimum to Uncle Sam. I realize you're here for golf and not business and was hoping we can exchange cards and perhaps I can call you next Tuesday at 4 p.m. for a follow up.

In both scenarios Harvey was not expecting to meet Jack, and Jack did a nice job of blending business with pleasure. Being a successful business owner, Harvey knows that many deals are made on the golf course. Jack struck a nice balance in a few ways: He asked for permission to proceed, he let Harvey know he knew who he was, and he praised him for his business success, carefully tying in his value proposition and how it may be beneficial for the two of them to have a follow-up meeting. In the second scenario Jack politely, respectfully, and subtly let Harvey know he was sensitive to the fact that Harvey was there for pleasure. Jack came across as confident, knowledgeable, and empathetic.

Situation 4: Making Contact with a Referral (someone you know through a mutual friend)

Jody, an account executive for an executive search firm, is at a friend's house for a party. In conversation she told Charlie, the host, that she is looking to expand her business. Charlie suggested she reintroduce herself to Ray, a mutual friend. Jody and Ray are now talking. They have gotten through the pleasantries and small talk.

Option A

*"Ray, I work at Berkshire Search. We place IT profes-
sionals in small and medium-sized emerging technology companies in the Northeast Region. We are known for our quick
turnarounds and as the only firm in our business that has a
100-percent guarantee on our fee for a full year. I am happy
to tell you we've never had to pay it back. Charlie told me
you were very resourceful and I should speak to you about
an opportunity to work with your company. Do you have a
few minutes to talk business now or should we schedule a
time and day for me to follow up?"*

In this scenario Jody was very clear about what she
does and what separates her company from the others,
and she has leveraged the relationship they both have with
Charlie to satisfy her objective in a nice disarming manner. Remember: Your *SuperNetwork* will open doors for
you that you couldn't on your own.

Option B

*"Ray, I work at Berkshire Search. We place IT profes-
sionals in small and medium-sized emerging technology companies that work specifically with Department of Defense
contractors. We are known for our quick turnarounds and
as the only firm in our business that has a 100-percent guarantee on our fee for a full year. I am happy to tell you we've
never had to pay it back. I am looking to expand our business and Charlie suggested you were very resourceful and
could help me and that I should reach out to you. Do you
know anyone in this vertical I described that I could talk
to?"*

In this scenario Jody altered her pitch by being very
specific and made it easy for Ray to think of whom he
knows in those industries that she may be able to call.

Again, it was simple and easy to understand because she was very clear about what her objective was.

Situation 5: Trade Show and/or Conference

Rob is a sales representative for D. Rothschild, an electronics distribution company headquartered in New Jersey that sells name-brand audio and video equipment to retail stores throughout the United States.

Option A

"Hi. I am Rob Wagner. I am in sales for D. Rothschild. We are recognized as the premiere consumer electronics distributor in the U.S. We are known for our focus on customer service, competitive pricing, brand selection, and quick turnaround. Some of our clients are Best Buy, Target, and BJ's Warehouse. What brings you here?"

Option B

"Hi. I am Rob Wagner. I am in sales for D. Rothschild. We are recognized as the premiere consumer electronics distributor in the U.S. We are known for our focus on customer service, competitive pricing, brand selection, and quick turnaround. Some of our clients are Best Buy, Target, and BJ's Warehouse. I am here to make contact and identify five potential new opportunities. What do you do for Circuit City?"

In both scenarios Rob painted an excellent picture of who he is, what his company does, and his company's distinguishing characteristics. In Option A, he used a probing question to satisfy his objective. In Option B his objective was similar to the one Hope had in the business-after-hours example.

Create Your Own Elevator Pitch

Record the main points you want to use in your pitch and create a script that effectively articulates what you want people to know about you and what you want to accomplish. Remember to reference the examples and incorporate the information from your completed self-analysis.

You will find that you will be customizing different pitches as things develop. As you saw from the examples in the previous section, you will need to slightly alter your objective based on the situation, opportunity, and type of person you meet.

Use the lines below to jot down some ideas for your elevator pitch. Then, in a separate notebook, create your elevator pitch.

_____

_____

_____

_____

_____

Most Commonly Asked Questions About Elevator Pitches

Q: Is it proper to sell yourself directly? Or just imply your skills?

A: Sell yourself! Being able to articulate your own skills is a basic skill.

Q: Should you avoid things people don't understand? Technical concepts?

A: Ask them—and quickly! In the first sentence, "Do you know about____? No? Then I won't bore you with the details...." Or "Do you know about____? No? Would you like to know a little more about it?" The bottom line is to make your pitch simple and put it on a level with which the audience can connect.

Q: What do you say if the person tells you she's not interested or can't help you?

A: Depending on the circumstances and or relationship, ask her, "Do you know anyone who might?"

Q: What's the goal of the pitch?

A: Provide a mental picture of who you are, what you do, and why you're talking to them. Again, remember what your objective is. What do you really want to accomplish?

Q: Isn't it rude to just talk about myself?

A: No. However, it *is* rude not to ask about the other person's interests, listen, or give the other person a chance to speak. What is important is that you start with the pleasantries first and keep your comments short. Include something you've heard about him as part of your pitch. It's a great way to break the ice and it involves the other person without handing over control of the conversation.

Q: How do I involve the other person in the conversation?

A: After you give information, ask a question. For example, after you say, "I work for ____," continue with the question, "Have you heard of us?" The person might say no, but you've gotten her involved and checked to see if she is engaged in the conversation.

Q: **How do I ask people for things without them starting to hate me?**

A: As a salesperson, you're always asking for a favor. You have to be comfortable with that. You have to be clear and to the point. Additionally, you have to give back when appropriate. Offer favors to people as often as it makes sense so they realize it's a give-and-take.

Q: **If I don't know a person, how do I keep from being too formal?**

A: If it's a social engagement, don't start right off with your pitch. Just say hello first and smile. Ask questions. Being genuinely interested in the other person will create an opportunity where he will eventually ask about you personally or professionally. Be patient.

Q: **What if I ask someone if I can call her and she says no?**

A: You could ask again and see if she still says no. This will show her that you're very passionate and committed. You might want to say something such as, "I'm sorry. Did I do or say something wrong?" or "I hope I haven't offended you because that wasn't my intent. Would it be okay to call you next week?"

Q: **I see someone I want to talk to, but I am having some fun or relaxing at the time and figure I'll catch him later on. Is that right?**

A: No. Don't ever do this. You don't know what can happen later. The person could be leaving to catch his son's ball game. He could be engrossed in other conversations later. He could be planning to leave early for any number of reasons. If you see an opportunity, take it right away!

Q: What if I truly only have a second and the target prospect will then be gone?

A: Give it your best shot. But make sure whatever you say gives her a really compelling reason not to leave. If you truly only have a second, you have to stretch that into a few more to ask for a meeting or get a card.

◆ ◆ ◆

Congratulations, you are out of the gate. I told you it would require some work on your part, but now you are on your way. Let's make sure you are ready to go forward. Go through this checklist and see if you can put a check next to every statement. If you can do that and say yes to each of these questions, you are ready to proceed to Chapter 2. If not, you need to go back and complete the exercises. Remember: The program has a building block approach. You can't shortcut the process. Think of it as building a house: It needs to have a solid foundation and be built brick by brick.

❑ I have completed my self-analysis.
❑ I now have a focus, or a better idea of what distinguishes me and my company.
❑ I now know the importance of having an effective elevator pitch.
❑ I have created my own elevator pitch that articulates an objective and articulates what my target audience needs to know to help me.

You are starting to get clarity and focus about finding better and more qualified sales and opportunities. That's good, because most people are "all over the map" and very vague. You are not. Let's move on.

Chapter 2

Draw a Road Map to Success:

Follow the Plan for the Outcome You Desire

Joan works as an account executive for an advertising company. She works in an open area. She hangs up the phone, gets out of her chair, and says to her colleague, "Give me a high five. I just got us a meeting at Sid's Club."

"How did you pull that one off?" her colleague asked.

"I have a former client, Ned, who works in public relations for them. I have not spoken to him for a while, but they are on my radar. I called Ned last week and explained that I am still focused on working with retail stores and had an interest in working with his company. He mentioned to me that he's not responsible for advertising and I should contact Melissa Perry, VP of marketing. I just called Melissa and mentioned Ned's name. She said Ned had called her about me and had great things to say about me and our company. I asked a few questions, listened, and then told her why I wanted to see her. She said yes."

You are thinking, *Networking isn't so hard. I just call people, tell them I am looking to expand my business, they give me names, I follow up, and pretty soon I have more appointments and the business will grow.* Wrong. Networking to get names without a purpose is an exercise in futility. You will be just spinning your wheels. No referral will really be able to help if you can't articulate exactly what you want that person to do for you. If you don't know where you are going, all roads will take you there. That's why you have to make a plan.

If you do everything prescribed in this chapter, you will get where you want to be and be working on only warm calls, receiving better and more qualified leads, scheduling more appointments, and closing more business in far less time than you ever imagined. Your peers and competition may think they know how to network. Do you know what they have going for them? They just have a list of contacts. That's all. What they don't have is a plan.

Before you pick up the phone to call anyone, you need to be prepared. You can't just "wing it," rely on your instincts, and hope for the best. A good referral is pure gold— and these referrals are likely to be the people who open the door to your next big sale. Your first conversation with your contacts and referrals is critical, and the objective of this chapter is to put you in the best possible position to get the response you want every time you call. Again, you never know when it could be—that defining moment that could immediately improve your sales results.

This chapter will give you a plan and all the tools you need to make a big impression on each contact or referral and to motivate these people to help you. You are going to make it so easy for these people to help you that it will not feel as though you're being an inconvenience or causing a hardship for them. You will be able to articulate and demonstrate your value proposition so well that the contact or referral will feel very comfortable helping you.

Do you have a strategy for every sales call, or do you "wing it?" Go ahead, be honest with yourself; there is no one else around. Most successful salespeople have a clear objective and a sound strategy to support it. Let's put this into a sports analogy to help explain what I mean. John Wooden, the most successful coach in college basketball history, had an objective for every game, which was to win. His record includes an .804 winning percentage over a 23-year period and 10 NCAA championships, including seven in a row from 1966 to 1973 at UCLA. He used different strategies depending on the opponent. He made sure his players understood the game plan strategy beforehand. He attributed his success to always having a strong strategy when he said, "Failing to prepare is preparing to fail." He may have lost a few games, but he always was prepared. For you it is the same. If you have a sound strategy of the type of new business opportunities you want to target and a clear objective, you'll make it easy for people to open doors for you, and you'll become very busy working on only warm calls.

Plan Your Strategy

We will now work on creating an effective road map to ensure that you get focused, identify the profile of account(s) you want to target to make it easy for people to help you, and get the outcome you desire from every call. Following this strategy will help you prepare for each individual call you make.

There are four steps involved in planning your strategy:

1. Evaluate your current position.
2. Consider what to do differently to bring in more business.

3. Determine what makes the most sense.
4. Put the action plan together and execute.

Write down your answers to these four steps on the summary form at the end of this chapter. Here's an example to show how you might proceed. The bullet points that follow are generic to help you start thinking about your own situation. Whether you are a small business owner, junior salesperson, senior salesperson, account executive, or sales manager, you may find that these bullet points describe your world.

1. Evaluate your current position.

- Industry pressure has kept margins tight.
- Competition is consistently under-pricing us.
- We have trouble differentiating ourselves in the marketplace.
- We are an industry leader, are the envy of the competition, and have significant differentiators.
- Prospective clients view our industry as a commoditized business.
- We have an aggressive sales quota and feel challenged every year to "raise the bar."
- Our industry company was #1 last year and want to be #1 again this year.
- I am new to the company and/or business.
- We have a great product but a weak marketing division.
- It is harder to find new opportunities.
- Customers are more demanding and less loyal.

2. Consider what to do differently to bring in more business.

- ◆ Start leveraging off my existing network of contacts to develop new contacts and help me open new doors.

- ◆ Continue to provide outstanding service and ask my clients for referrals.

- ◆ Focus on smaller accounts where I can get a better margin and quick turnaround.

- ◆ Focus on larger accounts so I can work on fewer relationships and bring in more revenue dollars.

- ◆ Become a niche player with a specific vertical (manufacturing, pharmaceutical, retail, financial services, and so forth), become known as the "go-to person," and start leveraging those relationships to open more doors for warm calls.

- ◆ Ask clients for more of their business.

- ◆ Make clients aware of our other service offerings or products.

- ◆ Develop a network database and prepare a plan to stay in touch with contacts on a more frequent basis.

- ◆ Attend more business-after-hours functions and network more with stated goal for a number of new contacts to be established weekly.

- ◆ Perfect my elevator pitch so I can be more effective when meeting people.

3. Determine what makes the most sense.

You might choose a few of the previous suggestions, and that's okay. Here are some other options, too.

- ◆ Identify the top 300 employers in our territory and begin leveraging our network of contacts

to get to the "right person" inside those targeted prospective companies.

◆ For quarterly visits with clients, bring an
"agenda letter" with action items and a "to
do" list (including maybe an evaluation or a
standard Quality Control form) and ask specifically for two to three referrals to help
"open more doors" with a warm call.

◆ Speak to client contacts and identify their
other vendors (who they use as suppliers) and
start to attempt to partner with them. See if
they are part of other associations, do they have
access to CFOs, or other verticals, and so on.

◆ At the beginning of the new year, meet with
"base customers" and have them invite up-
per management to the meeting. After establishing a relationship with them, follow up in
two weeks and ask for other senior level referrals to expand our network of contacts list.

◆ Target centers of influence (well-connected
individuals) and begin attending outings (golf,
wine tasting) to meet more CPAs, attorneys,
and so forth to nurture those relationships,
get more active in their associations, and get
an opportunity to work with their clients.

◆ Start giving keynote speeches at events and
conduct a program on a specific area of expertise to gain more exposure and develop
additional contacts.

◆ Contact a minimum of five contacts and clients each week and ask for at least two referrals from each contact.

4. Put the action plan together and execute.

It's one thing to come up with great ideas (as you will do in steps 1–3), but what will separate you from the others is your ability to execute. This is well stated in the summary title of the best-selling book by Larry Bossidy, former Chairman and CEO of Honeywell International, *Execution: The Discipline of Getting Things Done.* Executing the *SuperNetworking* plan to perfection requires discipline, too. Implementing your strategy will go a long way to contributing to your overwhelming success.

Here is where you prepare a time line for some of your best options. Some of your best options may start immediately but will require you to perform them on either an everyday, weekly, monthly, or quarterly basis in order to become a new habit and approach to sales strategy. Here's an example:

Strategy Time Line		
Action Item	Targeted Date	Date Completed
Work on new Elevator Pitch	17-Jul	17-Jul
3 weekly customer meeting to get referrals	24-Jul	Ongoing
10 referral calls to get contact in Financial Service Cos.	8/20/2005	
Go to Monthly Networking functions BC Club	5-Sep	

Joan, from the beginning of this chapter, was successful in getting the meeting at Sid's Club because of a few specific reasons. Her strategy was to focus on retail accounts where she can leverage her experience and relationships. She was able to clearly articulate to Ned what she wanted to accomplish and made it easy for him to help.

Because of the strength of their relationship, Ned made a call to Melissa on her behalf. The power of *SuperNetworking* provided Joan the warm call, an opportunity to get her voice heard by the right person.

Set Your Call Objectives

When networking it is very important to have an end result clearly in mind before you venture out to a networking function/trade show/conference, socialize, or make each call. Remember: You want to make it easy for people to help you. That's why you needed to have an objective as part of your elevator pitch. Before you go to a function or make the call to a contact or referral, you must ask yourself the following questions:

✦ What do I want to accomplish in this phone call or visit?

✦ What do I want to accomplish by going to this event?

✦ What do I want this person to do on my behalf?

Your call objectives need to be well-thought-out. Reaching each objective should trigger another event or action step that should be as specific as possible in order to maximize this contact's ability to assist you.

These objectives need to be:

✦ **Clearly defined.** In order for people to help, you must be very clear about what you want to accomplish.

✦ **Narrowly focused.** Get specific. Create that mental picture of exactly what it is you want the other person to do for you. If it is too broad it will be difficult for people to help. As an example you might say, "I am looking for contacts with large bio-tech firms in Bergen County. Do you know anyone I can speak to that works in a company such as that?" If you tell people you want help to get more clients and ask if they can help, they probably won't help. They may have a Rolodex of 1,000 people but, because your objective was too broad, you are making them work too hard to help you.

◆ **Quantifiable and measurable.** Your objectives need to be specific, such as an actual number of new prospects you want to meet, an actual contact name you want to obtain, or an introduction to two decision-makers you want someone to set up on your behalf. This is the only way to determine if you are getting the maximum return on investment of your time for any networking initiative.

Write down your objectives on the summary form at the end of this chapter. Here are some samples of call objectives for functions and making networking phone calls or in-person visits:

◆ Meet five CEOs.

◆ Receive two new leads.

◆ Receive six additional referral names.

◆ Get the name of a decision-maker at a prospective client company.

◆ Establish 10 new contacts.

◆ Pick up five new targeted prospective clients.

◆ Schedule a face-to-face meeting on your behalf.

◆ Make a phone call to open a door with a specific prospective client.

◆ Schedule eight new sales appointments.

◆ Make an introduction on your behalf.

◆ Arrange a future callback with a specific day and time.

Meet as many people as possible would not be a good objective. Remember that your objective can't be broad and needs to be quantifiable. Set realistic goals.

Paul attended an association's national conference in New Orleans, Louisiana, that had 350 attendees. He was there for two days and had objectives of leaving with five new sales opportunities and to close two pieces of business. He left the conference with only two new sales leads and did not close any business. Was that a successful trip? Some might say that two are better than nothing. As he evaluated his return on investment, he made the decision that he would not attend this conference again. Perhaps he set his sights too high and had unrealistic expectations. That may be true. Sometimes you don't know beforehand. That's why it is important to set objectives that are aggressive but realistic, to increase the likelihood your desired result will be achieved.

I was recently working with an organization that produces Wine Expositions throughout the United States. A part of its sales strategy was to send its marketing team to other trade shows to solicit exhibitors for its own shows. The results to date were disappointing. The return on investment was not good, and the organization was considering cutting back on attending some of the shows scheduled for the remainder of the year. I asked a simple question to Meagan, the general manager: "What is generally the objective when the marketing team goes? In other words, how many new leads do you expect them to come back with?" Meagan told me that they never had set measurable objectives when attending these events before, so I suggested a few quantifiable objectives to consider for future events.

They were planning to send two people the next day to attend a conference in San Francisco. We assigned each person a goal of identifying 10 new sales prospects and asking each of these new contacts for at least one additional referral. That meant Meagan's team was expecting to have 40 new sales opportunities to pursue. The following week Meagan called to tell me her salespeople came back with 60 new leads, and a week later I learned they closed five new accounts. Meagan told me that having a good strategy and clearly stated objectives made a huge difference, and they applied their new and improved elevator pitch that clearly articulated their value proposition with a stated objective. Do the necessary work, and you will make a favorable impression, get the outcome you desire, and make it easy for people to help you, too.

Now that you have reviewed a few examples, take a few minutes to complete your own strategy by filling out the following Summary Form.

Summary Form

Call Strategy:

_____

_____

Current Position:

_____

_____

Examples to Consider:

_____

_____

Best Option:

_____

_____

Execution:

_____

_____

What do I want this person to do for me?

_____

_____

What do I want to accomplish during this call?

_____

_____

If my initial call objective can't be met, what is my fallback objective?

_____

_____

List your call objective(s).

1. _____
2. _____
3. _____
4. _____
5. _____
6. _____

◆ ◆ ◆

Have you completed your networking strategy and objectives? If you just shook your head no to any of these questions, take a few minutes to reread the parts you skipped and complete the forms. Remember: You are building your *SuperNetwork* link by link. In order to have a solid foundation, you must follow the directions.

Chapter 3

Peel the Onion:

Find the Right Person Who Can and Will Help

Last year Andrea Mitchell, a news correspondent from NBC News, was on *Meet the Press* discussing the capture of Saddam Hussein. She kept referring to how the Army kept "peeling the onion" to get to the right person, a family member that would lead them to Saddam Hussein. Think about it for a minute. The Army had a specific target (Saddam) and a specific goal in mind (capturing him dead or alive) and determined that the best links to him were through his immediate family. They peeled the onion until they got to the core, to the *right* person who could and would help. Along the way, they made new contacts and referrals that they added to their list who helped them immediately, but who also will help them in the future. They were *SuperNetworking*, and it worked!

Everyone has a network. Whether you have contact information stored in your head, a shoebox of business cards, a Rolodex, a Palm Pilot, or a telephone book, you know people. For some, the list could be in the hundreds, and for others less. You need to build your list properly and then your contacts will help you get to the right person who can help you. Think of building your network of contacts as a bank account: You will get out of it what you put into it.

What you need to do now is create your contact list, and then I'll show you how to categorize and manage this list appropriately.

Who Should Be on My List?

Do not put just anybody on this list. What you have to do now is start thinking about the people who can help you expand your business. You don't want just any name, but rather people who can and will help.

- ◆ **Family.** Don't just think of immediate family. Think of your extended family, your brother-in-law's sister, and your distant cousins.

- ◆ **Close friends.** These are the people you are close to, whose friendships you value. These are people you can always count on.

- ◆ **People you know through others.** These are people who didn't make your "close friend" list. They are the people you are friendly with and who you feel comfortable asking for a favor.

- ◆ **Clients.** These are people with whom you have done business. Over time, you have established a good rapport with each of these people. You would feel comfortable calling any of them for a favor, and you feel confident they would give you a positive response.

◆ **Prospects with whom you haven't done business.** These are people you have never done business with for reasons beyond your control, but whom, over time, you have developed and maintained some sort of relationship. Even though you haven't done business with them, there is mutual respect. You may have similar interests, such as sports, or you have some things in common, such as having kids the same age. You'd be surprised, but they will help.

◆ **Vendors.** These are people you know because their companies have provided services to you. Vendors are also companies with whom you have worked, including your printer, advertising company, staffing firm, and security or cleaning firm.

◆ **Associations and clubs.** These are people you know through trade-related associations; chambers of commerce; golf, tennis, or swim clubs; a local PTO, Mason, or Rotary group.

◆ **Professional contacts.** These are people with whom you have developed some kind of professional relationships, but never really established a personal one. They could also be people with whom you are working or have worked in the past. These are people you know through associations or conferences you have gone to over the years.

The conversations you will have with people on your list will be slightly different depending on the type of relationship you have with each individual. The way you speak, what you say, and the type of intimate details you share regarding your current situation will vary. What you tell your brother will be different than what you would say to a vendor. That is why you need to categorize this contact list appropriately into four different levels of contacts: A, B, C, and D. Organizing it into a format makes it easy to maneuver.

Categorize Your Contact List

Your "A" list should consist of people you consider "heavy hitters," or well-connected. These are people you think are powerful in their business areas. These people are ones you think can "make things happen" by making phone calls on your behalf. These people come from any one of the lists noted previously. They could be business owners, presidents, CEOs, CFOs, COOs, vice presidents, or other high-visibility/high-profile personalities.

Your "B" list should consist of people from your family, close friends, and people you know through others lists. These are people with whom you can have candid conversations and on whom you know you can rely.

Your "C" list should consist of people you know through customers, vendors, associations and clubs, professional contacts, and competitors' lists. In addition, add to this list your lawyer, doctor, accountant, stockbroker, and your life insurance salesperson. Consider how many businesspeople they know. I am confident they can help you, too.

Your "D" list should consist of people who you wouldn't think at first could help you at all. This might sound odd at first, but your "D" list people are those who are not particularly powerful, but who just might know the "right" person you are looking for. An unlikely connected "D" list person might be your physical therapist, dry cleaner, butcher, or tailor. Let's take your physical therapist as an example.

Your physical therapist works with people recovering from injuries and surgery. On average, physical therapists spend 30 minutes with a patient, meeting approximately 80 people per week. What do you think people talk to their physical therapist about? The answer is simple, if not obvious: They speak to people about their families, what's going on with their life, and work. Can you imagine how many people this person knows? Do you think this person would refer you to someone if they simply knew what you were looking for? YOU BET!

My tailor, Benny, used to work for a fine men's clothing store. Ten years ago he went out on his own, and his customers followed. His business has grown, and he has an unparalleled reputation in the city of Boston. Benny's clients are predominantly senior-level people in different industries from financial services to hospitality, from entertainment to biotechnology. One day, Benny showed me his Rolodex. It was a "who's who" of the Boston business community. If I were looking for more financial services clients, I would call Benny before I would call anyone on my "A" list. Some of you might be thinking that I will not get my voice heard if I have to rely on the strength of the relationship my tailor has with this "big wig." That is the wrong way to think. First of all, everyone who knows Benny loves him. Secondly, Benny has great relationships with all of his clients. If anyone ever called me using Benny's name, I know I would pay attention out of respect for the relationship I have for Benny. That's how this works. People we don't often think of as a possible link can be an unexpected and invaluable resource.

Create a list of contacts and categorize them using the Contact List template on page 66.

CONTACT LIST

"A" List	"B" List	"C" List	"D" List

Now that you have a clear focus, an effective elevator pitch, and a comprehensive list of contacts, you are getting closer to the right person to speak with. In fact, you are probably closer than you imagined and you must simply think of building your *SuperNetwork* in terms of making the right connection.

6 Degrees of Separation Are Similar to Peeling the Onion

It has been demonstrated that we are just six people removed from anyone else in the universe. That means that, if you want to reach someone you don't yet know, you can do it by building the missing connections in your network to that person. These connections are built in two directions at once: from you to your target, and from the target back to you. For instance, if you are trying to reach the CEO of a company, you can research her bio, find what business school she attended, and go through your contacts until you find someone you know who went to the same business school. You are now just two degrees from the person you are trying to reach—or you only had to peel one layer until you got to the core, the right person. How you close the gap is one of the key secrets of *SuperNetworking*, and you will learn to master it in later chapters.

Using your *SuperNetwork* of contacts, you will soon find that you have access to people you never thought you would have access to.

I was conducting a workshop for a high technology firm in the Northeast where I explained this concept to 500 sales and marketing professionals at their annual sales conference. I told them that, through my network of contacts, I was six degrees of separation from anyone I wanted to access—and that they were, too. One participant raised his hand and challenged me to see if I could access George W. Bush, the president of the United States. At first there was some laughter in the audience, and then there was a hush in the audience waiting for the moment of truth. I thought about it for a few seconds and told the group, "I can access George W. Bush in three phone calls. In my previous life I worked in political fundraising in Massachusetts as the general manager for Eliot Savitz & Associates. In the late 1970s we worked on Republican campaigns, which were not very popular in Massachusetts at that time. Our founder, Eliot Savitz, worked very closely and became a friend of a well-respected, highly visible Republican state senator, Andrew Card. Mr. Card is President Bush's chief of staff. I am confident that a contact could be established. My call to Eliot would be the first call. His call would be to Andrew Card. That would be the second call. President Bush is his boss. Mr. Card calling the president on my behalf would be the third call."

Listen, I know that sounded pretentious. Some people at the workshop were rolling their eyes when I said I *could* reach the president. It's true and makes this important point: It is possible George W. would blow me off. However, it is a reflection of the power of *SuperNetworking*: I can access people or information easier or faster by leveraging my network of contacts. You can accomplish the same results if you put your mind to it. Whether it is targeting a company or person, start thinking about who in your network you know might be able to help get you started in the right direction.

The right person for you to contact is out there, too. It is very possible that your contact will refer you to someone else. You may find that this contact or the person she told you to call may not be able to help you with a specific company or person. Either way, you need to capture that pertinent information because, even though this person can't help you now, you may need her help at a later date. You just never know where your next opportunity is going to come from and how many people you may have to contact to get there.

Be Credible

Most people feel that because you use someone's name to open a door that it guarantees a successful call, or that, just because your contact makes a call on your behalf and now that you have a meeting or phone call set up with this referral, you will automatically get the business or help. Not true! The relationship you have with your contact to get your voice heard is merely a door-opener. Your credibility is on the line, and how you establish it with the referral is predicated by the way you conduct yourself during that initial conversation.

When you call your referral, you must come across as credible. There are three factors that you can use to establish your credibility:

1. Establishing a good reputation for yourself in advance.
2. Associating yourself with someone who already has credibility: your contact.
3. Conduct yourself well during the initial call.

Credibility From a Good Reputation

Although it's often true that "your reputation precedes you," this can be either a blessing or a curse. It's important to try to honestly assess how you are viewed by others. If your reputation is positive, the beginning of the conversation will probably go well. However, at this stage, your previous reputation will only have a temporary effect. Even the best reputation may be nullified if you don't make a good impression during the phone call.

Credibility by Association

By contacting a referral on the strength of someone else's reputation, you gain an opening to get your voice heard. The stronger the link between the contact and referral, the better that opportunity will be. Ideally, your contact will call or e-mail the referral first to set the stage for your call, but that's not always possible. Sometimes you don't want the referral to call on your behalf because he may not represent your interests properly. As with a good reputation, the effect of credibility by association is only temporary. To create a lasting positive impression, you must carry yourself well and be able to clearly articulate your message.

Credibility From Your Conduct

Earning credibility from your conduct is the only way to gain lasting and more permanent credibility. You must begin to earn it from the start of the first phone call by being articulate, clear, concise, professional, and courteous. A positive impression here will set the tone of your entire relationship with this contact and allow you to fully leverage the potential of this networking opportunity. Demonstrating your skill at networking is a selling point in itself, because people will assume that this is a reflection of your overall competence.

I have a friend, Seth, who knows many people in the retail industry and who I called to ask for help in opening a door for me at a particular company. I told him that I had finished developing a highly refined training system based on *SuperNetworking* that was being well received by my other retail clients. He not only said yes, but he sent a nice letter introducing me, and my company, to his contact, David, the director of compensation and benefits.

David was very friendly. He told me he was not the right person for me to speak with about my training curriculum and told me to call Dawn, the vice president of training, directly and to use his name as a referral. I called Dawn and we had a very good conversation. She asked me to e-mail additional information and told me to follow up with Bonnie in one week. Within two days of my e-mail I received a call from Bonnie, and the company is now a client. I know you are thinking this sounds too easy, and maybe you don't believe it. Well, it's exactly the way it happened, and here's why it worked the way I planned it.

I tied in my strategy and objective in a tight elevator pitch and made it easy for Seth to help me get the "ball rolling." Part of the definition of *SuperNetworking* is "identifying a specific target for a specific reason and figuring out the best links to get there." I was "peeling the onion" until I got to the core, the right person at the retail organization. Every time I used a referral's name to make a new connection inside the company, my credibility was on the line. Bonnie did not hand me the business because I knew Seth, Dave, or Dawn. But the bottom line here is that, if things are relatively equal and you arrived by way of your network and earned your credibility, you'll get the sale. Remember: Most times deals come together it's because *both* networks that have worked. And people like to do business with people with whom they are connected, even if it is an extended association, as in the previous example.

One key factor in gaining credibility is to demonstrate your understanding of the referral's company, industry, accomplishments, and interests. It is also essential that you be able to clearly articulate the value-added skills that you can bring to an organization and contribute to its future growth and success. Finally, your ability to confidently request what you would like the contact to do on your behalf will demonstrate that you are focused and in control. In Chapter 4 you will learn how to prepare for your referral calls so that you will earn your credibility, make a favorable impression, and get people to do what you want them to do for you every time.

Organizing the People You Know

When you begin working this program, you are going to find yourself extremely busy calling people, scheduling meetings, going on more sales calls, and constantly adding to your network of contacts. You need to keep everything together in one place so you can be more efficient and effective with your time.

It is important to capture the pertinent information in one place. Without writing it down in an organized way, you'll cease to be effective and things will start to slip through the cracks. Having a contact form to use as a guideline will allow you to track and organize your contacts.

You need to treat every piece of information equally, because you don't know which one could be the one that will point you to success, your next big sale. You cannot afford to lose track of even one piece of information. Every lead, no matter how small or where it came from, and even though it may appear to be a long shot, must be treated with extreme care.

One summer, I was with three other guys going to the beach. I ran into a woman I knew who was there with two friends. She told us the beach was windy and asked if we wanted to join them at a pond close by. As I tried to talk with one of the women during the day, I was picking up the vibe that she was not interested in me. As we were leaving the pond, her roommate asked if she could borrow my grill, and I said yes. I went to their apartment later in the week to pick up the grill. The woman who gave me the cold shoulder was there. We talked for a few minutes, and

I asked her for a date. She accepted. If I had not taken that next step, we would have never even spoken again. We have been happily married for 20 years and have three children. If we had not met that day and gone to the pond, my life would probably be different. You simply never know when an opportunity is knocking. Your next lead could be the one.

As we move forward, you are going to read about contacts and referrals. It is important that you understand the distinction, because the conversations you have with both will vary.

Contact: This is a person that you know directly. This is a person who you have put on your contact list because you have some type of relationship with. In addition, this is the person who tells you to call someone else to help you.

Referral: This is the person your contact told you to call.

Here's an example:

You called your *contact*, Michael Saltiz, told him you were looking to get into the Eleco Company, and asked if he knew anyone there. He said his good friend, Lou Lazar, worked there and suggested you call Lou using his name as a door-opener. Lou is now the *referral*.

While speaking with Lou, he said he was not the right person to speak with and told you to talk to Carl Berklund and Karen Carlson. At this point Lou became the *contact* and Carl and Karen are the...that's right, the *referrals*.

The sample format listed on pages 76–77 is a guideline for a repository to capture and store critical information you gather when adding to your network of contacts.

Defining the Fields

- **Contact.** Make sure you have the correct spelling for this person. Just because you know him doesn't mean you have the proper spelling of his name.

- **Phone number.** Make sure it is correct. Attention to this type of detail is very important.

- **E-mail address.** There are many ways an e-mail can go wrong because of its set-up. Be especially careful here. You obviously don't want e-mails going to the wrong person.

- **Referral(s).** Keeping track of these referrals is critical. If those referrals give you additional names, you would set up a place for their names in the Contact field. The names they give you to contact get placed in the Referral field.

- **Company.** This would be the company where your referral works.

- **Title, if known.** This would be the referral's title. You definitely want to get this information before you contact this individual.

- **Referral's phone number and e-mail address.** Same guidelines as for title.

- **Comments.** This is a very important field. You need to capture the essence of your conversation because, as you get busy, it will become almost impossible to remember every conversation you had. By capturing the information here, you will be able to refresh your memory and look at the chronology of all conversations you've had with an individual. You need to develop the habit of making careful notes immediately after you hang up.

- **Action to be taken.** This field will let you keep track of your actions. By recording this information accurately, you will always know the status of this particular relationship. As previously stated, it is *very* easy to lose track of things. Conversations are never as fresh in your mind 10 days later as they are just after they end. If you are working your network of contacts correctly, every phone call or visit will trigger a future activity. As more activity and action take place, this field becomes especially important.

◆ **Date of initial contact.** It is important that you enter the date for every communication you have. You cannot possibly keep track of the status of all your activities in your head. Timing is crucial, and you must be organized in that way.

Take your list of contacts and enter their essential information into the contact form, shown on page 76–77.

Getting the Most out of Your Contact Form

I would recommend the use of contact management software because it will remind you of when to call people and automate your process. Some software to consider, depending on your budget, includes ACT, Gold Mine, Siebel, and Sales Logix.

CONTACT FORM					
Contact	Phone #	E-mail	Referral(s)	Company	Title, if known
Michael Satitz	(508) 555-0000	Msaltz@ msn.com	Lou Lazar	Eleco	President
			Carl Berklund	Myte Security	VP of Finance
			Karen Carlson	System Works	VP of Marketing

CONTACT FORM (*CONTINUED*)			
Referral's Phone & E-mail	**Comments**	**Action to be taken**	**Date of Contact**
(781) 555-0000 laze@eleco.com	Michael gave me three names. He's calling all three for me to set it up.	1. Call Michael next week to see if he got through to everyone. 2. Call his contacts on the 2nd.	July 12
(508) 555-0000			
(978) 555-0000			

Go through this checklist and see if you can put a check next to every statement. If you can do that, you are ready to proceed to Chapter 4. If not, you need to go back and complete the exercises.

❐ I have completed my list of contacts.

❐ I have organized them appropriately into A, B, C, and D lists.

❐ I have taken the A, B, C, and D lists and entered all of their essential information into the Contact Form.

Where You Are Now?

1. You have a strong "elevator pitch."

2. You have a solid strategy and clear objectives.

3. You know who you want to call.

Do you think you are ready to call them? You might think so, but you still have a little more "front end" work to do. It's time to learn about conducting the necessary prep work you need to for your initial phone call.

Chapter 4

Paint That
Mental Picture:

Make a Great
Impression

Tom Riser was attending a keynote speech given by John Ziegler, chairman of AD&D Wireless. At first glance, AD&D Wireless appeared to be a good potential client for Tom's company, and if given the opportunity he wanted to make sure he would not miss his chance. Tom knew that if he got a chance to get in front of the chairman he couldn't just "wing it." Tom's chances for doing business with AD&D Wireless depended on making a good impression!

From doing his due diligence, Tom knew John's company was facing new challenges. When Tom finally got his chance after being introduced and exchanging pleasantries, he got right to the point: "John, I am aware of the challenges your company faces with the new 'Do Not Call' legislation and the new law that went into effect November 24th that allows wireless customers to change carriers and keep their phone numbers. I believe our training curricula can have a significant impact on your sales strategy when going after your prospects."

The chairman told Tom to send him an e-mail about his company and training and suggested that he follow up with a phone call in two weeks. Tom could feel the crowd building around them, and he was concerned whether or not John would remember him in two weeks. As he concluded the conversation, Tom said, "I will send the e-mail and follow up in two weeks. I will call you on December 9th at 4 p.m. I realize you are making contact with a lot of people here, and I hope you'll remember me. I am Tom Riser, and my company is Sell More." By now there were more than 50 people huddled around John, but Tom had taken advantage of his narrow window of opportunity. Tom was able to set himself apart by demonstrating that he had done some homework on John's company.

Do you think Tom has a good chance of at least getting a meeting with the appropriate people at AD&D Wireless to discuss an opportunity to do some business?

Absolutely! Your contacts are pure gold and should not be squandered. This means that you must prepare carefully for every one of your contact calls. Too many people assume that, because a contact is a close friend, she will automatically go out of her way to help. The truth is that, if you're not prepared when you ask even a close friend for a referral, not only is she less likely to make a referral for you, but her respect for you can take a plunge.

In this chapter, you will learn how to properly prepare before you pick up the phone to call someone. I'll also show you a strategy on how to gather critical information, where to get it, and how to match your and your company's strengths with your knowledge of the target company's "hot buttons" to calibrate your value to that target company. You need to do some research in order to come off as credible, to manage the call properly, and to get people to do what you want them to do. As they say in the military, you "need the G-2," the intelligence to make informed decisions. The same goes for top salespeople.

> *Nate was an account executive for an employee benefits company for more than 10 years and was well known in southern Connecticut. He wanted to expand his business in Westchester County, New York. In particular, he was targeting law firms because his benefits company was fairly high profile in Connecticut and had earned the reputation as the "go-to" brokerage company. Lori was the managing partner of a law firm with 100 employees and was someone who Nate wanted to reach. Their mutual friend Arnold had told Nate to call Lori and use his name to open the door. Nate got through to Lori quickly and said, "Arnold suggested I contact you. I'd like to send you a brochure about our firm's employee benefit program. Would that be okay?" And that's all he said. Because of the relationship Lori had with the mutual friend Arnold, of course she agreed. But what do you think Lori did when the information finally arrived? The envelope has still not been opened. Nate had not made a good impression on Lori. He had squandered the opportunity of a warm call.*

Here's a similar situation that had a different outcome:

> *Katherine received a call from Joe, who worked with her when she was in the staffing business. Joe had recently joined another agency that places accountants. Joe told her that he recently had seen a posting for a recruiting position with one of the world's largest office supply retailers.*

Joe remembered that Katherine used to do business with this office supply firm and asked if she still had any contacts there—and if so, would she be able to call on his behalf? Katherine made the initial call. Joe followed up a day later, spoke to the hiring manager, and demonstrated his knowledge and understanding about his business and position. He was able to secure an interview for two of his candidates the following week.

Joe had the same opportunity as Nate. But unlike Nate, he was able to make the most of that phone call because of a few specific actions he took before she made the call.

Let's retrace Joe's steps: First, he took what could have been a casual response to a Web posting and used his network of contacts to open the door for him. Second, his investment in conducting some up-front research on the organization and the position, along with the probing he did with Katherine to get a feeling about the personality of this individual, gave Joe a sense of confidence when he made the initial call to the hiring manager. Third, using his network, he was able to start at the top, separating himself from the hundreds of responses the hiring manager was going to receive for the job opening.

Now let's look at what Nate should have done. He should have been more articulate in giving Lori some direction about how he might help her law firm. He could have explained in more detail what he knew about the legal profession and the challenges law firms face with their employee benefit programs. He could have referenced other law firms his company services in southern Connecticut. He could have gotten more information from Lori by asking her about her firm and its current challenges. He could have demonstrated to Lori his experience with other law firms he works with and shown that he is knowledgeable about Lori's business. Had he done these things, Nate would have had a much better chance of getting Lori's business.

The lesson here is that getting an introduction to people is simply that: an introduction. That is all. How you prepare for the call and how you conduct yourself during the call will make the difference as to whether this person will help to open a door or meet with you. Effective presentations require skillful intelligence-gathering from your contacts, referrals, target company, and industry. Effective presentations also require a complete game plan of what you want to accomplish during the call.

Doing the Due Diligence

Before you actually pick up the phone to call or meet with any of your contacts and referrals, you need to look at each and every situation as a unique opportunity. You will need to go through a process that will allow you to come across as a person who is knowledgeable, resourceful, and organized.

I travel all over the country and work with all types of companies in various industries and ask a simple question: "How many of you conduct due diligence before your first contact with a prospective client?" To this day I have found that 90 percent do not conduct any due diligence. Thus, if you are carefully prepared, you will already be among 10 percent of all sales professionals who really distinguish themselves and make a favorable impression.

The up-front work you do will go a long way towards getting you where you ultimately want to be. You must do whatever you can to gather as much information as possible on the person and the company you are calling.

What Should I Know?

There are five basic questions you need to answer before you make the phone call:

1. What does this company do and/or what industry is it in?

2. Based on all the research I have done, it appears that this company needs help in which areas?

3. Based on what I know about the company and this individual, and my area of expertise, what are my value and my company's value to this company?

4. Who at this company or in this industry would recognize and appreciate our/my value proposition to the organization?

5. What do I offer that is quantifiable, measurable, and makes me and my product (or service) stand out from the crowd (both personally and professionally)?

Remember Gail, the sales representative who sold janitorial supplies who you were introduced to in Chapter 1? We used her self-analysis as an example. Gail identified a real estate company, M&G Properties, with which she wanted to work. She also had a friend, Dennis, who was a partner in that company and was preparing to contact him. Before she contacted Dennis, Gail needed to answer the same questions you will have to soon. Here is how Gail answered the five basic questions. There is also a short explanation of where you can gather/find this information in parentheses following each of Gail's answers.

1. What does this company do and/or what industry is it in?

M&G Properties is a commercial real estate leasing and management company.

(The answer to this question will either come from your knowledge or the research you will be conducting on this company. Research tips come later in this chapter.)

2. Based on all the research I have done, it appears that this company needs help in which areas?

Janitorial chemical supplies for their buildings and their tenants.

(The answer to this question will come from the due diligence you will conduct on a particular company. The source(s) of this information will be explained in detail later in this chapter.)

3. Based on what I know about the company and this individual, and my area of expertise, what is my value and my company's value to this company?

M&G Properties gets consistent delivery of service from an experienced company with more than 50 years that is knowledgeable in servicing real estate clients all over the United States.

With our size and our levels of expertise in particular areas, we have the resources locally and nationally to solve any facilities-related problem. With this one-stop approach, M&G Properties doesn't have to look elsewhere for any of its maintenance supply needs. Our expertise along with a "do whatever it takes" attitude to deliver the best and most cost effective materials keeps Dennis's properties always looking great.

(The answer to this question will come from your responses to the first two questions and from the answers in your self-analysis.)

4. Who at this company or in this industry would realize and appreciate our/my value proposition to the organization?

Dennis, because he is responsible for the day-to-day management of all properties, and his operations and property managers.

(The answer to this question will come from your due diligence or from your contact referral.)

5. What do I really offer that is quantifiable, measurable, and makes me and my product (or service) stand out from the crowd (both personally and professionally)?

No other janitorial-chemical supply company in the southeast can offer the variety of services we can. We have done this for other clients and we can show M&G Properties the cost savings and improvements. Our seasoned, well-trained, stable, and knowledgeable management team ensures efficiency, consistency, and service delivery second to none.

Dennis can count on me 24/7. When he buys from us, even though we are big, I am going to own his account. It is mine. I love taking over an account and making a big difference. I know the business. I know real estate. I know the demands. I am knowledgeable and will be there to support his account. I am prepared to provide reference accounts. I would offer to take Dennis and select members of his staff to either call or visit my accounts and have them talk directly to the clients.

(The answer to this question will be a culmination of answers to questions 1 to 4 and the answers in your self-analysis.)

I realize you might not be ready to answer these questions yet. The point is that you must understand the value of knowing about a company or an individual. Now you will learn where to go to gain this knowledge.

Where Can I Get This Critical Information?

There are numerous sources. Using only one of them may provide you with enough information. The more you know, the more of an edge you will have over your competition.

The person who gave you the referral.

This contact may be able to tell you a lot about the person you are calling. From a conversation with your contact, you can learn what the referral is like personally and professionally, as well as his family situations, interests, and hobbies. You may also gain some insight into what is going on in the company and what your target audience's hot buttons are. This way you can really have a meaningful conversation and capitalize on the relationship that exists between your contact and your referral. Remember the story about Nate and Katherine? It's clear that the time Joe spent with Katherine and the probing questions she asked about the hiring manager really paid off. Also, she asked Joe to call ahead on her behalf, which he did. Don't be afraid to ask your contact to make that initial call for you, too. The worst he can do is decline.

People you know that currently or previously have worked for or with the company.

These people will be able to give you tremendous insight into the company. This information should allow you to ask quality questions of the referral or contact. The type of insight you can get from insiders might include how the company is doing, how the company is viewed in its industry, information about its competition, what makes the company so successful, the company's culture and environment, and its future challenges. The types of questions you ask and answers you give your insider will send a strong message that you have done your homework and are different, and more qualified, than your competition.

People you know who are currently or have previously worked with your contact or referral.

Finding someone who knows the person who you're about to call is invaluable. Gathering information about your contact or referral from someone who has actually spent more than 40 hours per week with her will provide you with useful information on many levels. It will certainly help you manage the conversation and give you a real competitive advantage. Back to that situation with Katherine and Joe: She wanted to schedule a meeting and ultimately be able to submit a candidate for an opening and start doing business with him. Besides speaking with Joe, she remembered that someone she knew, Gary, used to work for the hiring manager. Even though Gary did not leave the company on the best of terms, Katherine called him. Katherine learned about the hiring manager's style, disposition, and expectations. When Katherine goes in for her initial meeting, she will have gained more insight into the company, department, and individual then probably any other salesperson soliciting them.

Here are the types of questions you want to ask your contact. In some situations, you may ask only a few.

About an Individual:
1. How well do you know_____?
2. Can you give me a little insight about _____'s personality?
3. What are _____'s interests outside work?

4. What do I need to do to earn _____'s business, trust, and confidence?

5. Do you know of anything I should stay away from?

6. How would you recommend I approach_____?

About an Organization:

1. What do you know about_____?

2. What do you think are its (or the person's) hot buttons?

3. Do you know anything about its decision-making process?

4. What do you know it looks for when working with vendors?

The Internet.

Technology has allowed us to gather a tremendous amount of information from the public domain. Just because you developed significant information from the people just mentioned, it is important that you get the big picture, too. There is information on the Internet about both companies and individuals. You can sometimes get a full background on the person you're going to be contacting by using this resource. In searching on the Internet for either individuals or companies, there are a few search engines worth mentioning to access information. They are:

- *Google.com*
- *Yahoo.com*
- *Hoovers.com*
- *AskJeeves.com*
- *AltaVista.com*
- *AOL.com*
- *MSN.com*
- *Search.com*
- *Bloomberg.com*

Company Website.

The information you gain from this source is invaluable. You must always check a company Website as a part of your due diligence regardless of the amount of other information you have accessed. This is the place to find the core information of what the company wants you to know about it. Here is where you should look on a company Website, and what you should look for:

- **Home Page** or **About Us.** This is a place to get a great overview about who the company is, what it does, and who its clients are.

- **Products and Services or Capabilities.** This will give you insight into what types of products and services it offers.

- **Investor Relations.** If the company is public you can look at its financial reports to view the size of its company and, more importantly, how well it is doing.

- **Media or Press.** It is particularly important that you cover this section. This will provide you with current happenings within an organization, such as new product releases, an acquisition, recognition in its industry, or a change in senior management. You want to acknowledge and discuss this information when you have a conversation with your contact or referral.

- **Management Team.** When looking at the management team you might recognize the name of someone you know who could become an important contact. Look at everyone to see if you can locate some kind of connection. Ask your network of contacts what they might know about a member of the senior management team. More often than you'd think you will find someone who went to the same college or perhaps worked at a company where you or someone in your network used to work. If you look hard enough, you can find a connection.

Here is an example of how digging a little bit can pay major dividends:

Beth was a speaker at the Quinnipiac Chamber of Commerce. Her topic was business etiquette. She met with someone from a regional bank who expressed interest in working with her organization. When Beth got back to the office she went on his company's Website. When she looked at the management team she recognized the executive vice president and thought he was someone she had played golf with in a pro-am tournament many years ago.

When Beth got home she went through her paperwork and found a picture from that day. She called the executive vice president the next day and told him about the conversation she had with someone else from his bank at the Chamber function. He offered his help and asked Beth to keep him apprised of her progress. That bank is now a long-standing client. The fact is this: You simply do not know where the connection is going to be made when building your SuperNetwork.

Competitors

Go to their Websites, too. See what the "other guys" are doing and how they represent themselves in the marketplace. Try to understand how your contact's company or your referral's company attempts to differentiate itself from its competition.

You want to demonstrate that, even though you are an outside vendor, you are a strategic thinker and ready to be part of its team. You might want to pick out something to discuss about its competition. This, again, is a great way to demonstrate to your target audience that you are different from 95 percent of the people that go after its business but invest only minimal effort on the front end. Your contact or referral will appreciate the way you have prepared yourself.

Here is a P.S. to the story about Beth:

> Peter, Beth's sales representative, was asked to meet with a prospective client, BPC, one of the world's largest power solutions companies. The company was considering Beth for a keynote speech and wanted to meet Beth in person. BPC also wanted Beth to give some of its executives a demo to assess the Business Etiquette program and her ability to deliver the content and determine if it was the right message the company wanted to send to its employees. Before Beth made her presentation she asked a few probing questions, which confirmed a lot of what she had learned while doing her due diligence. She demonstrated that she was familiar with the business, understood BPC's competitive environment, and was able to point out what its competitive advantages were.

> Beth also took some very educated guesses about what she thought were BPC's challenges, which were readily confirmed, and was then able to make clear where her company could help. At the end of the presentation BPC executives told Peter and Beth they would get back to them by the end of the week with their decision. It didn't take that long. By the end of the day

Peter received a call from his contact, Terry, who said that they were "so impressed with your knowledge of our business, our competition, and your insight into our challenges that you had earned their business." BPC is now a highly valued client of Beth and Peter.

Another reason why you want to look at the competition is because these companies might be of interest to you if things do not come to fruition with the company you originally targeted. This way, the investment you will have made into your prescribed industry of interest will potentially have an alternative payoff. Your time will not be for naught. As an example, Jacqueline, an experienced software sales executive from Tiebel, has a track record with financial services companies and now wants to focus exclusively on that vertical market. Her target account is Fidelity. She also did her homework on Putnam and Scudder, too. If things do not work out for her within a reasonable amount of time at Fidelity, do you think Putnam or Scudder will be getting her call? Probably. Based on her experience and initial due diligence she will eventually pursue them, further utilizing the time she has already invested.

User Groups

Birds of a feather do flock together. These are associations for people in your industry that sponsor programs for education purposes. People who are members of user groups pride themselves on having what I refer to as "course knowledge." That's a golf term for knowing the terrain of business, what obstacles to avoid, how to avoid them, and what you need to do to be successful. The internal fabric of groups such as this is "knowledge transfer." If possible, you should find the major user groups in your target area. Again, their insights into a company or individual may be invaluable. Just remember why you are asking for help in the first place: to gather information on an individual or company.

Trade Associations

These are very similar to user groups. Most professionals belong to some group. They use their membership to stay current on what's happening in the field, but they use it also as a networking forum. Members of a trade association often possess and share intimate knowledge about a company or individual, and they can become referrals or contacts for you to open up other doors into additional companies. If you are a member of any of these types of organizations, try to get the membership directory. Make sure you are judicious when using it. Remember that you want to be very focused in your approach. Just because you get a list (such as a membership directory) does not mean you should call everyone on it.

What Happens if I Contact Every Resource I Can Think of and Still Come up Dry?

Yes, of course that is a possibility. My advice is to get outside the box, challenge yourself, and not accept defeat. Put yourself into a mind-set that there must be someone that can get you this information. Push yourself past where others would have given up. I encourage you to try a little harder, and you may just open up a door you never imagined.

Here's a story where this challenge was raised in one of my workshops from someone who had been confronted with what appeared to be a dead end:

Anne Marie, a sales representative for Metals and Minerals company, was looking for more opportunities. She identified a bell manufacturing company that interested her and was located near Waterbury, Connecticut. This company had been around for 30 years and was privately held. The company did not have a Website and, after exhausting her network of contacts, she could not identify anyone she knew who could help her get access to company information or in the door. She was very frustrated because she could not get any additional information on this organization. I probed a little to see if we could find a few ways that she had not thought of that might have allowed her to "go against the grain."

Here were the options we developed:

- ✦ She could call the company to see if it had a brochure and have one sent.
- ✦ She could go to the Thomas Registry of manufacturers to see if the organization was listed and perhaps get the names and titles of the management team. If Anne Marie were to get the names, she could then work back through her SuperNetwork to see if anyone recognized a name.
- ✦ She could contact the Waterbury Chamber of Commerce to see if the company is a member. More than likely someone from the Chamber will know the principals of the bell manufacturer.

As we discussed these new options Anne Marie realized she had more avenues to pursue this opportunity. She was pretty sure that her contacts and other people she knew who worked and lived in the Waterbury area would be able to help her in her quest. She decided that using her contacts to go through the chamber of commerce made the most sense.

The point is that, even if you don't know anyone in the company, if you put together a strategy, you'll be amazed with what you can come up with. In Chapter 9 you will be introduced to the idea of having a mentor help you exceed your quota. The type of brainstorming session I did with Anne Marie is the kind of thing you may want to go through with your mentor. You may not have all the answers, and you are not expected to. However, if you put in the effort, the results will follow.

Dead in the Water!

I can't possibly overstate it enough that you can't just "wing it" when you call someone. Getting people to do what you want them to do is a reflection of how well you manage the phone call.

You might be having what you think is a successful phone call, but inevitably your contact or referral is going to ask one of these questions:

- ◆ What do you know about our company?
- ◆ What do you know about our industry?
- ◆ Do you understand what we do here?
- ◆ What do you know about me (or my situation)?

If you say "I do not know much" or try to bluff your way through, you will have, in all likelihood, destroyed your chances of success with the call in general and this contact in particular. You will lose all credibility with this person. More importantly, you will probably have "burned" this contact not just for this opportunity, but for future ones as well. In addition, when your name comes up in future conversations, this person will be unlikely to volunteer positive thoughts about you. As I mentioned before, you never know which contact will be the one to steer you toward your ultimate goal. You cannot afford to blow it by being unprepared. Remember: 90 percent of sales professionals don't do their homework, so it's not hard to stand out in this regard.

Once you have done the necessary due diligence, you should be able to complete these preparation questions for each person and company you contact. You will carry the answers forward in Chapter 6 when you are preparing your phone script. Choose a company in which you are interested; answer the following questions on a separate sheet of paper.

1. What does this company do and/or what industry is it in? (This will come from your due diligence.)

2. Based on all the research I have done, it appears that this company needs help in which areas? (This will also come from your due diligence.)

3. Based on what I know about the company and this individual, and my area of expertise, what are my value and my company's value to this company? (This should be a combination of your due diligence and your self-analysis answers.)

4. Who at this company (or in this industry) would realize and appreciate my/our value proposition in his or her organization? (This will come from your due diligence.)

5. What do I really offer that is quantifiable, measurable, and makes me and my product (or service) stand out from the crowd? (This should be a combination of your due diligence and self-analysis answers.)

Pop Quiz Time!

This chapter was focused on showing you the value of proper preparation, how and where to get that knowledge, the importance of making a favorable impression by gathering as much information as possible, the danger of not being prepared for the initial conversation, and the importance of discerning and articulating your value to a given company.

1. What percentage of people do the necessary due diligence before they speak to prospective companies?
    a. 10 percent.
    b. 30 percent.
    c. 50 percent.
    d. 80 percent.

2. Where are the best sources of information you can get about a person or company?
    a. The newspaper.
    b. A variety of sources including the Internet, company Website, referral(s), competitors, and Google.
    c. Myself, friends, neighbors.

3. "Dead in the water" means?
    a. A fish died.
    b. Man overboard.
    c. I was trying to "wing it" when I made a call and got stopped in my tracks when I was asked "what do you know about our company?" and did not have an answer.

◆ ◆ ◆

If you answered a to #1, b to #2, and c to #3, you are really paying attention and are now ready to apply what you have learned so far and proceed to Chapter 5.

Chapter 5

Polish Your Image:
Know the SuperNetworking
Do's and Don'ts

George, a C-level exec in an emerging technology company, was at Comdex in 2003. He knew it was the "place to be" to make contacts in the technology world and drum up business. Over the past few years he had developed outstanding relationships by attending. This year he wanted to do more. His objective was to identify six target companies with which he wanted to do business. One of his targets was Bell Computers. He was ready to spring into action. While rekindling an old friendship, he suddenly noticed a representative from one of his target companies sitting nearby. He politely excused himself from his conversation with his old friend. He walked over the rep and gave him his elevator pitch. They spoke for five minutes when George, sensing the conversation was going well, seized the opportunity and said, "Mark, I noticed you were talking with one of your colleagues, Jay Beck, before I came over. I would really like to meet him. I think there is real synergy between our respective companies and would appreciate the introduction. Can you do that for me now?"

At this point in the book you have invested a significant amount of time on developing effective elevator pitches, sound strategy and clear objectives, specific target(s), earning credibility, and proper preparation. Remember: You will only have one chance to make a favorable impression. Do you think George made a good impression and was able to meet Jay Beck? Not only did they meet, but they spent more than an hour at an after-hours networking function and got to know each other well. Jay is now a client of George's, and they have become good friends, too.

Every contact you make could be that magical one where you make a sale, get the million-dollar contract, or embark on a relationship that fuels your company's future growth! You can't blow it on something that seems irrelevant. You must work to be savvy about what you say, what you don't say, and how you conduct yourself in any networking endeavor. It doesn't matter whether it is getting on the phone, meeting with a contact, referral, or prospective client, or attending a function, before you start *SuperNetworking* your way to future growth and success you need to be sure you are observing some essential do's and don'ts.

Essential Do's

Smile, Make Strong Eye Contact, and Extend Your Hand First

You want to set the proper tone and begin the conversation on a positive, friendly, and professional note.

Ask Questions and Get to Know People

People like to talk about themselves. By showing a genuine interest, you will learn a great deal about them and begin to earn their trust. Also, they will begin to like you because they think you have similar interests.

Remember Your Elevator Pitch

Keep it short and sweet.

Always Ask for a Business Card Before Giving Yours

This is subtle but very important. It shows that you really are interested in the other person and are not just trying to hand out as many business cards as possible.

Make Notes When Receiving a Business Card

After you have met someone, exchanged business cards and moved on and write a quick comment on the back of the card. You might write something about your conversation, an interest (such as "likes golf") or connection, a follow-up item, what he looks like, or a promise you've made to him. If you've gone to function or trade show and go back to your office with numerous cards, it is impossible to remember every conversation you had and match it up with the name on the business card. Making notes will help.

Making a Connection Helps

If you meet someone for the first time and start having a good conversation, or perhaps run in to someone you know who can introduce you to someone you want to meet, ask for an introduction, just as George did. Remember: A warm introduction is better than approaching an individual cold. If the opportunity presents itself, offer to return the favor. You've heard that expression "birds of a feather flock together." The warm introduction gives you temporary credibility. What happens after that is up to you.

Attitude, Attitude, Attitude

People can sense your mood, whether in person or over the phone. People gravitate to positive people. Your positive attitude is contagious, infectious, and helps make a great first impression. If you are feeling discouraged, worried, upset, or angry, or you are distracted, it's detectable. Only attend functions or make phone calls when you are feeling positive and upbeat, and work on being able to control and change your attitude quickly so you're not held hostage to it.

Carry Yourself as a Winner

Although Michael Jordan may not have won every game he played, he always carried himself as a winner. His swagger and tone of voice tell people that, win or lose, this guy is a champion. You need to carry yourself the same way.

Speak With Confidence

Let people feel your energy, passion, and interest. Show some energy and excitement without going overboard.

Use Inflections

Make your points with vocal variety and hand gestures for emphasis. Don't speak in a monotone. If you aren't sure how your voice sounds, use a tape recorder to find out.

Remember: It's Just a Phone

If you feel intimidated, the phone will feel as though it's a 20-pound barbell. But if your confidence level is high, it will be light as a feather.

Ask for Action

Former Speaker of the House Tip O'Neill always said, "People like to be asked, and people like to be thanked." He learned that lesson the hard way: He lost his first election because he didn't ask people for their votes. You can't afford to make the same mistake. You must ask for your referral's help and then hold him accountable for the commitments he has made. Don't hesitate to call back a few times to make sure that he fulfills those commitments.

Always End the Conversation on a Positive Note

Make sure the referral leaves the conversation feeling good about helping you.

Essential Don'ts

Don't Be Unprepared

Know your audience beforehand. Make sure you have done all of your "due diligence," as previously described. If you are attending a function and there is a guest speaker, do some due diligence on the person, company, and industry. Call the sponsors beforehand and try to gain as much insight as possible, possibly get an attendee list to see who is attending, and possibly check their Websites. Do as much as you can, go into any function prepared, and you will separate yourself from the other attendees.

Don't Forget Your Business Cards

Have your business cards in various pockets so people do not see bulging cards and it doesn't appear as though you have brought your old baseball card collection in your jacket pocket. If you have a card wallet, use it.

Don't Inflate Your Ability

You are who you are, so be comfortable with it. If your audience can sense that you are not being honest, you will do more harm than good.

Don't Fail to Listen

Pay attention to what is being said. People can sense it when you're not paying attention. If all you want to do is talk and aren't both listening and giving the other person an opportunity to be an active participant in the conversation, you will lose him.

Don't Cut People Off Mid-Sentence

If you cut people off, they are going to think, "*Gee, this person does not listen, and is rude, too.*" Keep in mind that you are asking this person to help you. If you repeatedly cut the referral off mid-sentence, you make a bad impression and are unlikely to get the help you are seeking. If there's a point that you don't want to forget, write it down and bring it up when there is a break in the conversation.

Don't Under-Respond

If you give too much information, your audience will think, "*This person rambles on.*" If you provide too little information your audience will think, "*This person lacks depth.*" You must be thorough and to the point in order to make a favorable impression.

Don't Share too Much Information

You don't need to give your audience your life story. You don't want this person to think, "*That's really more information than I needed.*" You will lose people's attention if you give them too much information. You have a strategy and a clear objective. Do not stray from your objective.

Don't One-Up People

Be humble. People get turned off whenever someone constantly is trying to top whatever it is the other person does, says, or has.

Don't Talk Negatively About Other People or Companies

Negative talk is counter-productive and sends the wrong message. Further, what if this person has friends in that company or knows the person you are talking about, but has a much higher opinion of the individual? It might sound like a long shot but, believe me, it happens! Play it clean and smart.

Don't Be Afraid to Ask the Tough Questions

Don't start thinking, *I better not ask 'why?'*. Asking the tough questions will get you closer to your goal and will help you figure out whether this person will be able to help you. Capable people will respect you for asking the questions others would avoid. For example, let's say that your due diligence shows that this company's CEO resigned. You absolutely should ask about it. You will not only get the answer you need to properly evaluate the company and come up with an effective sales strategy, but you'll also differentiate yourself from other potential vendors who don't have the confidence to ask such a tough question. Most sales professionals don't ask the hard questions and make assumptions for answers. Assumptions do not equal either answers or truth. It's very dangerous to assume anything—just ask the question.

Don't Apologize for Asking for a Favor

You want to come across as a confident, self-assured person. It's okay to show your appreciation. People appreciate the display of common courtesy. When you're networking to expand your business, it's perfectly acceptable to ask for help, so don't apologize for doing so. As long as you maintain a polite, professional, confident manner, most people will respect your requests. Remember that networking is a two-way street and that someday you may be in a position to return the favor.

Don't Let People "Off the Hook"

Hold people to their commitments. Polite persistence wins out every time. You might have to call people a few times in order to get them to do what they said they would. Don't be shy, even if you are. Remember: This is your book of business. It's too important not to give it your all.

Do a Post-Call Debriefing

After every networking initiative, whether you attend an event or making a phone call, you need to take a moment to figure out whether it was successful and what you have accomplished. Immediately after the networking event, ask yourself the following questions:

- ◆ Did I accomplish my call objective?
- ◆ Did I reach my goal for the call?

It's up to you to set your expectations of what you are trying to achieve. Your objectives need to be clearly defined and narrowly focused so when you conclude you'll know right away whether you have reached your call objective. Consistently achieving your short-term objectives will quickly move you forward to your ultimate goal.

Are You Ready to Get on the Phone?

1. Do you know what it means to "peel the onion?"
2. Have you done your due diligence?
3. Do you have a call strategy?
4. Do you know what your call objective is?
5. Do you have your profile completed?
6. Are you prepared to ask the tough questions and not let people "off the hook"?
7. Do you know what to avoid doing?
8. Are you prepared to have a call debriefing to determine whether your call was successful?

If you can answer yes to all of these questions, you are ready to prepare your phone scripts. If you answered no to any of these questions, take a few minutes to reread the part(s) you may have missed. Remember that you are building your *SuperNetwork* link by link. In order to have a solid foundation, you must follow directions.

Chapter 6

Hold Their Feet
to the Fire:

Extract Promises
and Commitments

Brian, an agent for NJ Life, wanted to land a new account with a successful surgeon who lived nearby. His friend, Jeremy, introduced them at a party. Brian was preparing what he would say during the follow-up phone call. Brian wanted to make sure he got this doctor's attention and get an appointment. During the phone call Brian decided to use a little humor when delivering his value proposition by saying, "I'm known for being the most candid life insurance rep in this community and I promise you if we ever work together, I will never tell you about my health issues unless I become your patient." They both had a good laugh. Brian went on to say, "When we were together at Jeremy's house we agreed that I would call you today at this time to schedule a time for us to meet to discuss your short-term and long-term life insurance needs. What's a good day and time for you next week?

By now I am sure you have realized you can't just "wing it" in order to effectively and consistently achieve the outcome you desire when speaking to your network of contacts to help you expand your business. In order to get the best results, your future conversations must be managed in a certain way to extract promises and get your clients, contacts, and referrals to do what it is you want them to do for you.

Preparing Effective Scripts

At this time, you have completed the necessary preparation to make a successful call resulting in increasing your network of contacts and bringing you closer to your goal of generating more business for you and your company and making more money. You have figured out what your profiles of target accounts are and whom you want to call. You have a successful strategy, know your call objective, have done your due diligence, and are finally ready to get on the phone. If you agree with this statement, you are ready!

Because you are about to get on the phone and ask for a favor, you need a strong sales pitch. Every effective sales pitch has certain elements designed to steer the conversation in a way that ensures the outcome you desire. What you say, how you say it, and the easier you make it for people to help will go a long way in determining how successful your conversation will be.

There is no better time than the present to start reaching out to your network of contacts. What you are going to learn in this chapter is how to develop an effective script. You will be shown several time-tested sample scripts to use as guidelines that you can tailor to fit your own personality. These sample scripts are much more of a guideline than an absolute rule. You need to blend these samples into your own style when creating your script. You must feel comfortable with whatever comes out of your mouth.

People can sense when you are reading a canned speech. (Can't you tell when the telemarketers call your house? You just want to hang up because you can tell they're reading. Don't let that happen to you.)

Alex, the experienced financial advisor, and Gail, the junior salesperson, will reemerge in this chapter. You will review their sample scripts and also a transcript of actual live calls they made. Take the sample scripts, create a few that you feel comfortable with, and be yourself.

This chapter will provide you with the elements of an effective script of what to say and how to ask for help when speaking to clients, contacts, and referrals, covering:

- ◆ Utilizing information gathered from your self-analysis, due diligence, strategy, and call objective.
- ◆ Articulating to the client, contact, or referral why you are calling.
- ◆ Articulating a clear understanding of what you want them to do for you.

As defined earlier, clients, contacts, and referrals are different people. The way you approach them must be different also. You will learn how to hold them accountable, ensuring your phone call will result in moving this process forward.

How will you know whether your phone call was successful? You'll know by conducting the call debriefing that was outlined in the previous chapter. You will be shown how to measure the success of your phone calls by going through a quick checklist that will indicate whether you were as effective as you thought you were.

Let's start by putting together a script when you're making a call to a client and contact.

Your initial call should:

- **Be focused and specific.** Use the information from your self-analysis.
- **Have a stated reason for the call.** What do you want this person to do for you?
- **Be succinct and clear.** You must give people a road map so they can help you. If you are vague or lack clarity, your likelihood for success will decrease. Just ask Nate from Chapter 3. If you can clearly articulate your interest in a concise manner, people are more likely to start thinking of others they know in that field or like companies and individuals they can recommend you contact.

Phone Call Scripts When Speaking to a Client or Contact

You need to give your client or contact a clear idea of what type of company or industry or profile of an individual you are looking to access. You may ask him if he knows a particular person, or the "right" person, to contact at a specific company. The key here is that you are not looking for just *any* name, but you want to get to the "right" person. You must make things as clear and simple as possible, because few people are going to spend large amounts of time with the process if you do not make it easy for them to help you. You need to create a mental picture of exactly what it is that you are looking for. If the idea doesn't come to him quickly because you haven't positioned things properly, this avenue of networking won't be optimized. Remember: You want to get him excited about what you do and the value you bring to potential clients, your approach, and the benefits of your service or product. You are going to ask contacts and referrals for favors and potentially put their reputations on the line in order to help you. They need to feel 100-percent confident the person they are recommending is excellent at what he does.

Here are the essential steps that you need to follow (in chronological order) when speaking to a contact or client. On the following pages we'll review each step in detail so you'll be in a position to achieve your desired outcome.

1. Setting the stage.
2. Showing that you value his time.
3. Setting expectations.
4. Triggering a reaction.
5. Generating activity.
6. Closing the loop.

1. Setting the stage.

Start the conversation by exchanging pleasantries and make sure you ask about the other person. Slow yourself down. You don't want to come across as desperate or as only being interested in having her help you. After you get through the pleasantries, here are a few examples of things you might say:

For contacts

"I would like to talk business and could use your help."

"I am looking to expand my client base and would like to ask for your help."

"I am looking to expand my business relationships, and I could really use your help."

"I need your help. I am looking to expand my client base and wanted to talk to you about it."

For clients

"Your business is very important to me, and I want to make sure everything is okay these days. I could use your help."

"Your business is very important to me, and I value our relationship. I want to make sure you are happy. Is everything okay with our services these days? Great! I could really use your help."

"Our relationship is very important to me. I appreciate your business. Do you mind if I ask for a bit of help?"

"I am looking to expand my client base and would like to ask for your help."

2. Showing that you value his time.

Make sure you have his undivided attention. Always ask if this is a good time to speak with him. You want to make sure your client or contact is paying attention and appreciates that this is important to you. If this person is distracted in any way, you won't get the undivided attention you need to get the most out of this contact. Most callers fail to ask this question and simply leap ahead into their speech only to find out the person is busy or rushing out to a meeting. You will have lost all momentum and, if you get a chance to repeat your spiel later on, your chances of success will have greatly diminished. Don't let this happen to you. You may also want to ask for a specific amount to set a reasonable level of expectation.

Same for both clients and contacts

"Do you have some time to speak with me now? If not, will you have a little bit of time in the next day or two for

us to speak? Or should we reschedule at a time that is more convenient for you?"

"Have I caught you at a bad time? If so, we can reschedule for a better time."

"Did I get you at a good time?"

"Do you have a few minutes to speak with me now?"

3. Setting expectations.

Let her know what you are looking for; be very specific. You will take the information you completed in your self-analysis and apply it here. Help her visualize exactly what your target profile account is either by mentioning profile of individual specific companies, types of companies, size of companies, industries of interest, or geography. If you create this mental picture for your contact, she can start thinking of people she knows or companies she is aware of that could benefit from being introduced to you. It is very important that you are not vague here. Most people feel they should be broad so they do not limit their opportunities. In reality, that has the opposite effect: It makes it harder for someone to give you a referral. Take a look at these:

Same for contacts and clients

"I am looking to expand my client relationships with Fortune 500 companies in the Chicago Loop area."

"I am looking to expand my book of business and want to make contacts at the highest levels with more corporate headquarters within a 30-mile radius of Denver and the suburbs. Our sweet spot is medium- and large-sized companies with more than 100 employees."

"I am looking to expand my client relationships with more colleges in the Mid-Atlantic."

"I am looking to expand my client relationships with more hospitals in Boston, in particular Beth Israel Hospital. I was hoping you could introduce me to your friend Cheryl Nyland; I learned she is the head of Purchasing for BI."

4. Triggering a reaction.

Put his feet to the fire (and maybe flatter him a bit). Here is where you let him know what you want him to do for you. Do you want him to give you some other leads, or names of people for you to contact? Do you want him to help you open up a door at his company or another company? Remember your call objective, and stay focused on what you want to accomplish in this phone call. People have an ego, and you are asking for a favor. Don't hesitate in stroking his ego, as it may help him go further out of their way to help you. You might say:

For contacts

"I was hoping you could help me out. You have always been a great resource in the past. I was hoping you could provide me with the names and contact information of at two to three people I could contact?"

"You are so well connected and seem to know everyone in your industry. Do you think you could give me the name and contact information for the buyer at Jerry's Furniture?"

"I noticed that MicroTech is on the move and, because you know the owner of the company so well, I was hoping you could set up a meeting or call him on my behalf."

"I'd like to grab a quick lunch with you soon to fill you in on what's happening here and see what you think. At that time I'd like to pick your brain to see if you could provide me with some ideas of companies I should target."

For clients

"I was hoping you could help me out. I would like to provide the same outstanding service to other successful business owners of privately held companies locally. I was hoping you could give me the name and contact information of at least two to three people I could contact."

"I was hoping you could help me out. I would like to offer the same array of products and provide the same outstanding service to companies such as _____. Do you know anyone that works in any of these companies I mentioned?"

"I was hoping you could help me out. You have always been so complimentary and offered to help in the past. I would appreciate it if you could provide me with two to three people that you know in a similar position as you that would want to benefit from having an association like ours."

"I was hoping you could help me out. I remember you introducing me to Christine Patterson last year at your golf outing. I would love to speak with her about our comprehensive investment management programs. Do you think you could set up a lunch meeting for the three of us to get together?"

5. Generating activity.

Your phone call, if managed properly, is going to force your contact to react in some way. She is going to help or not. If she offers to give you a few names or make a phone call on your behalf or gives any other positive response, proceed to step 6. It is possible that she will not be able to give you a name for a variety of reasons. The following are some likely scenarios and how you should respond to them.

For both contacts and clients

"I can't think of anyone now."

Your Response: "This is really important to me. Do you think you can take some time and reflect on our conversation, and I will call you back on Thursday at 4 p.m. and maybe you will have had time to think of a few people I can contact?"

"No."

Your Response: "Do you mean no, you won't help me, or you don't know anyone? As I mentioned before, this is really important to me and I could use your help."

"I don't know if they have a need for your services or product."

Your Response: "I am not asking you to do any soliciting on my behalf. I'm really just asking for your help in identifying companies that might be a good fit based on the criteria I described to you as a target account. You know my style and sales approach. I won't be too pushy, unprofessional, or aggressive It's up to me to do the legwork and find out if we are in fact a good fit for them."

"I have not spoken to Frank in a long time. It would be a stretch to call him."

Your Response: "I'll call. I am really looking for help to open a door. What's the worst Frank can say when I call him and mention your name? If he says he can't or would not help, I'll just move on. That's the worst that could happen. You know me well. I would never do anything to embarrass you or jeopardize our relationship."

"I am not really comfortable giving out a name. How about I give him your name and if he's interested, he'll call you?"

Your Response: "Part of the power of networking is strength of the referral. I would never do anything to embarrass you or jeopardize our relationship. With all due respect, I believe that no one else can articulate what we do and how I can help_____ better than I can. This is really important to me and I would ask that you reconsider."

6. Closing the loop.

You got a positive response, so you set yourself up for another "warm call." Your client or contact offers to give you a few names of people he knows. Those people are referrals. That's great! Now you want the referral call to go just as well. Part of the reason this last call went well was because of all the preliminary work you did as described in Chapters 1–5. The other reason is because you have a solid relationship with your client or contact. Now you want to get the client or contact to call the referral on your behalf and start a solid new relationship for you with referral.

This way the ice will be broken and it will be a warm call, making it much easier for you. Try one of these:

For both contacts and clients

"Do you think you could call Joe on my behalf?"

"Do you think you could call Joe on my behalf and give him a heads-up so he will be ready to take my call?"

"Do you think you could call Joe on my behalf and give him a heads up so he will be ready to take my call? As you know, a warm call is more effective than a cold call."

"Do you think you could call Joe on my behalf and give him a heads-up so he will be ready to take my call? As you know, a warm call is more effective than a cold

call. And your calling him ahead of time makes it that much easier for me to get the conversation started."

◆ ◆ ◆

Here are two sample phone scripts from Gail and Alex you can also use as a reference when preparing your own:

Transcript #1: Gail Calling a Contact Asking for Help Expanding Her Business

Gail: Hi Len, it's Gail. How was your vacation?

Len: Great. The golf at Hilton Head was excellent. The water was warm and every day was 75 degrees and sunny. How are you doing?

Gail: Pretty good. I hope I'm as lucky as you with the weather next month when my family and I head to Disney World. Listen, if it is okay I'd like to talk a little business and ask for your help on something. I realize that because you just got back you may be busy. Do you have some time to speak with me now? If not, maybe I can call you back in the next day or two so we can talk?"

Len: Now is a good time. What's up?

Gail: I am looking to expand my client relationships and sell more floor wax products into other property management firms in the greater D.C. area. I was hoping you could help me out. You have always been a great resource in the past. I was hoping you could provide me with the names and contact information of at least two to three senior level people you know in property management whom I can contact.

Len: Sure. Give me second.... Call Greg White at Sterling Properties at 555–555–1234. You can call also Gina Russo. Remember her? She used to be with us and moved over to Capital Management about nine months ago. She can be reached at 555–123–5555.

Gail: Can I tell them you suggested I call?

Len: Sure. Just let me know how it goes. Gina is a good kid. I think you guys will hit it off.

Transcript #2: Alex Calling a Client Asking for Help Expanding His Business

Alex: Hi Chris, it's Alex Bell. How have you been?

Chris: Fine. How about yourself?

Alex: Great. Your business is very important to me, and I want to make sure you are happy. Is everything okay these days?

Chris: Fine. As a matter of fact, I am glad you called. I can now cross you off my list. I was very pleased with the new statement your analyst sent me. I can zero in on things quicker and feel much better about the asset allocation. Let John know I said thanks.

Alex: I will do that. By the way, I could use your help. Is this a good time for us to speak, or should we schedule something at a time that is more convenient for you?

Chris: Now is a good time. What can I do for you?

Alex: I am looking to expand my client relationships with other successful business owners such as you in Orange County. I was hoping you could help me out. I would like to provide the same outstanding service and full array of services to help other people you know that you think would want to benefit from having me involved in their financial planning. I was hoping you could provide me with the names and contact information of at least two to three people I could contact.

Chris: Alex, I've got to tell you I am a little uncomfortable giving out names. People don't like that. Besides, I have no idea what some of my friends are doing with their financial planning, and I don't want to get them mad for giving out their name.

Alex: I realize financial planning is a private and sensitive manner. I have built my practice on the strength of relationships I have developed over the years just like the one we have. Please know I would handle each conversation with the same care, discretion, and approach I took with you when Fred introduced us. Would it be possible for you to give this more thought? I would like to call you next Tuesday to see if perhaps you may come up with some ideas. Would that be okay?

Chris: Sure.

When Alex called back he got the referrals.

◆ ◆ ◆

Following are some last-minute reminders before you create your own script.

- **Don't use the phrase, "*Do you know of any companies that may have a need for my product or services?*"** Avoid asking questions that can get an easy "no." You risk ending the conversation quickly. Also, you may lose the connection for future requests.

- **People want to help.** Just ask.

- **Fear is your friend.** It's okay to be a little nervous calling these people. Stay confident.

- **Be prepared.** Do not shortcut your due diligence, strategy, or objective for each and every call. Use the guidelines presented in this chapter and customize every call.

Now it is time to create a script for yourself.

Phone Call Script
(Contacting a Client or Contact)

You are calling a client or contact to ask for a referral. (Use separate sheets of paper as necessary.)

Set the Stage.

_____

_____

Get Their Attention.

_____

_____

Value Their Time.

_____

_____

Set Expectations: Let Them Know What
You Are Looking For.

_____

_____

Trigger a Reaction and Generate an Activity.

_____

_____

♦ ♦ ♦

Phone Script When Speaking to a Referral

Because you were so effective when speaking with your clients and contacts, they gave you names of people to call. Now you want to be able to leverage the relationship between them and the referrals and get the referrals to do something—whether it is to meet with you, give you another name, have them introduce you to someone in his companies, or help you in some other way. By managing the conversation correctly, these referrals will also become contacts for you as you continue to peel the onion, going through the layers until you get to the core: the right person who can help you.

The way you approach the referral is slightly different than the technique you used when calling your clients and contacts. As always, how you conduct yourself when speaking with the referral will leave a lasting impression and directly affect the outcome of your call. In Chapter 3 you learned about credibility. Using someone's name to open the door gives you temporary credibility when the conversation gets started. It does not mean this person will definitely will help you. Earning more permanent credibility will be dictated by how you conduct yourself throughout the entire phone conversation, which will have a bearing on whether this person will help.

The essential steps that you need to follow (in chronological order) when speaking to a referral are listed here. As we did with the steps when speaking to a client or contact, we'll review each step here in detail so you'll be in a position to achieve your desired outcome.

1. Grab her attention.
2. Value his time.
3. Break the tension.

4. Have a definitive positioning statement.
5. Set expectations.
6. Trigger a reaction.

1. Grab her attention.

You need to quickly establish why you are calling. You must, of course, mention your client's or contact's name up front to get the referral to pay attention and listen to you. You may want to say something along the lines of:

"You and I have not spoken before. Rachel Zack asked me to give you a call."

"The reason for my call is your neighbor Don and I were talking the other day, and he told me to call you directly."

"Last night I was at the Chamber of Commerce function and I was with Lauren Friedman, and she was telling me you about your company. She suggested I give you a call."

2. Value his time.

Make sure you have his undivided attention. Just as you learned about calling your client or contact, always ask if it is a good time to talk. You want to make sure your contact pays attention to what you say and that he knows the referral is very important to you. You can't tell if someone else is in his office, if he is in the middle of a project, if he might be about to leave the office to go to a meeting, or any other reason why he cannot give you the time and attention you need at that moment. Try, for example:

"Is this a good time to speak with you? If not, we can reschedule for a better time."

"Did I get you at a bad time?"

"Is this a good time for you? If for some reason you can't spend a few minutes with me now, please let me know and I can call you back at a better day and time that is more convenient for you."

"Is this a good time to speak with you? Please let me know and we can reschedule for a better time for you."

3. Break the tension.

Here is where you bridge your relationship with your contact into an "icebreaker." You could say:

"Mitchell told me to send his regards."

"When was the last time you spoke to Carol?"

"I hope mentioning Steven's name is a good thing."

"Melissa is such a good person, one of my close friends. I appreciate the fact she suggested I call you."

In the rare instance that this referral is not receptive to even a bit of small talk to break the tension, don't let that throw you off your game. Quickly explain who suggested you call and go right into your pitch:

"Kim told me to call you because...."

4. Have a definitive positioning statement.

This is where you talk about what distinguishes you and your company, your value proposition (from the work you did in Chapter 1 when completing your self-analysis and creating your elevator pitch). Combine that with your insight into your referral's company or industry (from the due diligence you did). This information will give referrals a mental picture of who you are and what type of opportunity you are targeting, as well as help them think about who they know, and how they can help.

You may say:

"I am sales rep for Telcomm Business Solutions. We provide best-in-class integrated solutions for business communications, offering a single point of contact for your local, long distance, and Internet services. Our sweet spot is medium- to large-sized companies in Rhode Island with more than 150 employees. Kevin told me a little bit about your company and, after I researched it, I believe there are synergies. We are both privately held, recognized as industry leaders, and recently acquired respected competitors."

"I am in sales for D. Rothschild. We are recognized as the premiere consumer electronics distributor in the U.S. We are known for our focus on customer service, competitive pricing, brand selection, and quick turnaround. Some of our clients are Best Buy, Target, and BJ's Warehouse. I understand you are an officer with the Consumer Electronic Association and know many of the senior buyers with the country's audio and video chain stores."

"I have been with DCDS for 10 years in sales. We are one of the country's largest health benefit providers. Some of my clients are corporate headquarters and university and hospital employees. We are known for our outstanding customer service, quality of products, and size of our network providers. While doing my due diligence I learned that you service the same type of clients."

5. Set expectations.

Here is where you ask for the referral's help. All calls should continue with, "I could use your help." Remember: People like to be asked and thanked. You could say:

"I could use your help. I am very interested in working with your company and would appreciate your help in introducing me to the right person. ..."

"I could use your help. Chris told me you were the right person to speak to in your organization about our service offerings (or products)."

"I could use your help. I am interested in working with other audio and video stores, and Gary said you were well connected and that I should introduce myself to you. Perhaps you could help me make further inroads into this market."

"I could use your help. Gary said that, because we both sell to the same type of clients, you might know where the best opportunities are right now. Perhaps we can share leads and help each other out."

6. Trigger a reaction.

Generating an activity. Most importantly, remember what your call objective is. What do you want this person to do for you? Here is where you put his or her feet to the fire and *ask for the order*:

"I would appreciate it if you could give me the name of your purchasing manager or make an introduction on my behalf."

"I would appreciate it if you could provide me with the names and contact information of at least two to three people you could think I should contact." Perhaps add, *"Could you do that for me?"*

"I would appreciate it if you could help me connect with Tara Berger. Would you be able to help me out?"

"I would welcome the opportunity to meet in person. Is there a good day and time for you in the next two weeks to get together?"

"I want to be respectful of your time so I'd be happy to meet you either before work, or maybe a quick bite after work—my treat. At that time we can get to know each other better. What's best for you?"

"Gary mentioned it would be mutually beneficial if we spent some time together and got to know each other better. Is this something we can schedule now?"

If there is any hesitation, your simple follow-up is this:

"Do you mind if I call you back in one week's time after you've had more time to think about it? At that time we can discuss this further and the best way you suggest we proceed."

Whether your contact does or does not call ahead of time on your behalf, you need to follow the steps outlined for the referral call. Alex and Gail will stay with you. Review their sample scripts and also a transcript of real, live calls they made. Again, take the sample scripts and create a few with which you feel comfortable, and be yourself.

Sample Referral Scripts

Referral Transcript #1

Gail is contacting a referral, and the contact has not called on her behalf. She is calling Gina Russo. Her objective is to get a meeting with the right person at Capital Management who is responsible for purchasing their cleaning supplies.

Gail: Hi, Gina. You and I have not spoken before. Len Baker suggested I give you call. Is this a good time for us to speak?

Gina: Depends. What's this about?

Gail: Len and I were together yesterday, and he told me to send regards. He is a client of mine. I work with Spectro supply in Reston. Do you know anything about us?

Gina: Only by name. Why don't you tell me a little bit about your company?

Gail: Based on what I know about your company from my due diligence I thought it would be important for you to know we are the largest privately held chemical supply company in the SouthEast with more than 50 years servicing real estate clients all over the United States. What distinguishes us is our quality of products, expertise in your space, the resources locally and nationally to accommodate all of your properties in the U.S., rapid response capabilities, competitive pricing, and a "do whatever it takes" attitude to deliver the best and most cost effective materials ensuring your property looks great every day so you look good to your tenants.

Gina: What do you know about us?

Gail: That you are a growing company and have made numerous acquisitions in the Northeast and now have more square footage under management than any other property management firm headquartered in the D.C. area. With that growth I believe we can be a real asset to your organization because we have offices in every state you are in.

Gina: Sounds interesting.

Gail: I could use your help. Len told me you would be able to help me find the right person to speak with about your commercial building and mall cleaning supply needs. Do you think you could put me in touch with the right person?

Gina: I could. You are talking to that person now.

Gail: Well, I guess Len knew what he was doing when he suggested I call you! I would welcome the opportunity to meet with you in person and get an even better understanding of your current and future needs and challenges.

Gina: Okay.

Gail: What's a good day and time for you the week of August 2nd?

Gina: Why don't you come in on Tuesday, August 3rd at 10:00 a.m.? Do you know where we are?

Gail: Yes, I do. August 3rd it is. I will let Len know we connected. Thanks again for your time. I look forward to meeting you in person in a few weeks. Take care.

Referral Transcript #2

Alex is contacting Sandy, whom the contact, Chris, has called on his behalf. Alex's objective is to get an appointment with this business owner.

Alex: Sandy, this is Alex Bell. Chris Dunn told me he called you on my behalf and suggested I contact you directly.

Sandy: Yes, he told me you would be calling.

Alex: Is this a good time for us to speak?

Sandy: As good a time as any.

Alex: Chris told me you were his golf partner in your club tournament this year.

Sandy: Yup. I had to carry him, as always.

Alex: Well, I don't know how much Chris told you about me. I work at Burell Finch as a financial advisor. We are the largest independent investment management firm in New England, helping clients grow, protect, enjoy, and transfer wealth. I only work with business owners of large, multigenerational families providing the highest levels of confidentiality and integrity in our industry. I have studied your company from afar and was very impressed with what you have done with the organization over the last two years.

Sandy: Chris spoke very highly of you. But I am all set in that regard.

Alex: I understand why you might have said that. With all due respect, Chris felt the same way before we started working together. Chris thought it would be mutually beneficial if we met. I would welcome the opportunity to spend some time with you and give us a chance to get to know each other a little better. I realize business owners such as yourself do not put all their eggs in one basket. Perhaps as I gain a better understanding of what your long-term financial goals are I can make a few recommendations to help you reach your objectives, without any obligation on your part other than some time spent with me. Would you be interested in getting together and getting to know each other better?

Sandy: How much time do you need?

Alex: Initially one hour. I will then need to come back and provide you with the detailed analysis based on our initial discussion, and that should take another hour. Two hours total.

Sandy: Let's book it now for next Tuesday at 9 a.m. in my offices and I will make a determination at that time whether we will have the follow-up meeting.

Alex: Thank you. I look forward to meeting you in person next week.

Phone Call Script (Contacting a Referral)

Use the due diligence information you gathered from the example you completed in Chapter 4. Use additional paper as necessary.

Grab Her Attention.

_____

_____

Value His Time.

_____

_____

Break the Tension.

_____

_____

Have a Definitive Positioning Statement.

_____

_____

Purpose for the Call.

_____

_____

Trigger a Reaction. (Some calls should continue with "I could use your help.")

_____

_____

◆ ◆ ◆

Listen, Listen, Listen...

Just because you have an awesome script does not guarantee that the conversations you have with your contacts, clients, and referrals will be successful all the time.

The reason is because the words you speak, though extremely important, are only part of the equation! Your ability to *listen* is the other, and it is a huge factor in determining your success or failure.

Throughout this process of calling people and "peeling the onion," your contact or referral does not always respond the way you would like or expect, and you may start to doubt the strength of the relationship. Don't panic! This is not at all uncommon. Whether your call is a good one or bad one, if you are not listening to what you are told, you will not be able to respond properly, ascertain a next step, or realize where the future opportunity is. The people on the other end of the phone do not have the benefit of seeing your script and certainly don't have one of their own. Having a great script, combined with your ability to listen and respond properly, are the key ingredients to a successful call. Remember this: You can't have one without the other.

...and Then Give Yourself Some Feedback

Your conversation will lead to some sort of reaction. What this means is that another activity or action will follow based on the particulars of that call. You must go through the following checklist before you pick up the phone to make additional calls to determine whether your call was a success.

❑ Did you personalize and customize your call?

❑ What was your call objective?

❑ Did you make it easy for this person to help?

❑ Did you remember not to let him "off the hook"?

❑ Did he commit to do something for you?
❑ Was your call objective satisfied?

If you can put a check next to each question, good—that means you *did* have a successful call, though you still have more work to do.

```
Just Do It!
—Nike
```

The biggest frustrations clients have with sales professionals is their lack of consistent follow-through and follow-up. Whatever needs to be done, make sure you live up to your commitments. This will determine the kind of long-lasting credibility you will have with referrals, which will go a long way towards determining how successful you will become. Ultimately, and most importantly, it will impact how big and how strong your *SuperNetwork* will become. You are constantly being evaluated on what you say and do. Take care of business.

Leaving Voice Mail That Gets Attention

Any voice-mail message needs to be brief, peak your recipients interest, be informative, and trigger an action. The type you leave for a client or contact will be different from the one you leave for a referral. What follows are time-tested examples that ensure that people either call you back or prepare them to receive your next call. Either way, these will guarantee that you will be speaking to them soon.

Sample Voice Mails for a Client or Contact

"Dana, this is Britney. I need to speak with you. Could you please give me a call when you get back to the office?"

"Dana, this is Britney. I need to speak with you. If you get this message before the day is out could you please give me a call at home around 8 p.m.?"

"Dana, this is Britney. It is important to me that we connect before the week is out. I will try you again tomorrow morning. If that doesn't work for you, please let me know by phone or e-mail what's best for you."

Sample Voice Mail for a Referral

"Hi, Frank. This is Britney Graham. Dana Cooper suggested I give you a call. I can be reached at 508-555-1213 later today and tomorrow. If that's not good for you, I will call you back on Friday morning at 10 a.m."

"Hi, Frank. This is Britney Graham, Dana Cooper's friend. I am calling at Dana's request. Dana thought it would be a good idea for us to connect. I would appreciate it if we could speak by the end of the week. If it works for you I am around between 8 and 10 a.m. tomorrow. You can reach me at 508-555-1213. If I haven't heard from you by Thursday I will call you back on Friday at 2 p.m."

"Hi, Frank. This is Britney Graham. I had lunch with Dana Cooper earlier today and she told me to call you directly. I could use your help and wanted to schedule some time to speak when it is convenient for you. I am around the rest of the day today and can be reached at 508-555-1213. If I have not heard from you in a few days, I will call you back on Friday at 2 p.m."

Gatekeepers: The Administrators Who Keep You Away From the Person With Whom You Want to Speak

It is so important to develop a rapport with these individuals. These people are trained to keep people away from their boss. It is part of their job description. However, these people are also human beings and generally will respond better to people who treat them with respect and not disdain. That is why you should always ask for their name and let them know you really need their help. This will disarm most. If that doesn't work, mentioning your client, contact, or referral's name should neutralize them. They generally have no idea how well your client, contact, or referral knows the person you are trying to reach, or the relationship between them. The "gatekeeper" is fear-driven. Part of his or her responsibility is to allow a limited number of people access to his or her boss, When you mention your contact's name to access that boss, the gatekeeper may not know the origin or strength of the relationship. Therefore, he or she is more apt to be of assistance rather than run the risk of having his or her boss be disappointed with the way you were treated. Using this knowledge will get you what you need.

I had been working with a particular client for the past few years. The vice president of human resources, Ellen, is someone I have known personally for more than 20 years. Linda, her assistant, at first did a thorough job of screening my initial call. After a few conversations and a visit to the facility she learned about my long relationship with Ellen, and her tone and demeanor changed. Now when I call she immediately recognizes my voice and books our next appointment or conference call, and we have developed a relationship of our own. The power of using a client, contact, or referral's name will help you get through too.

Here is a transcript of a real-life conversation with a gatekeeper.

Admin: Hello, Darren Testa's office.

Lucy: Hi, this is Lucy White. Is Darren available please?

Admin: No, Darren isn't available right now. May I ask what this is reference to?

Lucy: Chris Dunn suggested I call. If you could let Darren know that Chris wanted us to connect, that would be great. Please have him call me tomorrow at 10 a.m. at 555–555–0948. If not, I can call back on Friday morning.

Admin: If he's interested he'll call you back.

Lucy: I can appreciate that. I could really use your help. Chris said it would be important that I speak to Darren this week. Do you think there would be a better time for me to call him back?

Admin: You can try back at tomorrow at 8 a.m. He's usually around to take phone calls at that time.

Lucy: Thank you very much. I'll call back tomorrow.

Admin: You are welcome.

◆ ◆ ◆

Did you notice how the administrator's tone changed as a result of Lucy's approach? The administrator was not going to cause a problem when Lucy made her understand there was a relationship between Lucy, a third party (Chris), and her boss. Use this transcript as a guideline if you find yourself speaking with a tough administrator.

Sometimes, though, the gatekeeper's tone does not change. Here are a few suggestions to overcome this obstacle:

◆ Ask if it is okay for you to e-mail the referral.
◆ Ask for the gatekeeper's name so you can reference him or her in your follow-up e-mail to the referral.

- Try back another day. Perhaps the gatekeeper was just having a bad day or you caught him or her at a bad time. Perhaps you can call back in a few days and get a better response.

- Call your contact and ask her to make a call on your behalf. It's possible that your contact knows the gatekeeper well enough and can help you move this process along.

- Call the referral either before 8 a.m. or after 6 p.m., when people are more likely to be answering their own telephone lines. Usually gatekeepers are not working at those hours.

When a Link in Your *SuperNetwork* Doesn't Perform

What happens when you reach the right person and you get the cold shoulder? Sometimes you will have what you thought was a great conversation with a referral and, for whatever reason, the referral has not responded the way you had hoped. Here are a few likely scenarios:

- You called the referral and you have not spoken directly with him yet. You have left a few messages without receiving a callback.

- You spoke to the referral and he was in a rush and told you he would call back, and you are still waiting for the call. Or he scheduled a specific time to speak to you again and you feel as though you were "blown off."

- You spoke to the referral, who promised to do something for you and who has not followed through on his commitment.

- You are speaking with the referral and your instincts tell you things are not going well.

◆ You are getting a bad vibe. And by the time you are off the phone, your gut is telling you this person is not going to help you.

Is It Me or the Referral?

It is natural for you to wonder if the problem is with the referral or yourself. You'll find yourself reflecting back on the call and trying to figure out if you did something wrong or didn't handle things right.

Don't doubt yourself yet. There's a good chance you didn't do anything wrong at all. It could be that the referral has been traveling or has been out sick and unable to get back to you in a timely manner. Perhaps the boss imposed some deadlines or she just forgot, even though they made a commitment to you. Any number of things could be going on in the referral's life that could impact her ability to help you.

What Should I Do?

Go back to your client or contact who gave you the referral. Explain the situation and see if the client/contact has any insight based on their relationship. Ask the client/contact to call on your behalf to find out what happened. This might give you an opportunity to get things back on track. This will also give you closure. If it was not *you* that was the problem, he will be primed for your follow-up call. If in fact there *was* something you did during the conversation that alienated the referral, learn from it and make sure you don't repeat the mistake. Then move on.

◆ ◆ ◆

Once you have prepared your own customized scripts, you are ready to get on the phone and make things happen. You now know:

- How to prepare an effective script when speaking to clients, contacts, referrals, and gatekeepers.
- What to say and how to ask for help to extract promises and get the outcome you desire.
- How to present yourself in a way that will get the client, contact, and referral to put you in touch with not just anyone, but the "right" person who can help you.
- How to leave an effective voice mail.
- What to do when someone gives you the cold shoulder.

These scripts are going to lead to great conversations, better and more qualified leads, and more revenue-producing activities. If you have been following along and have not cut any corners, you are going to get people to help, and you will be getting closer to the "right" person.

Chapter 7

Don't Drop
the Ball:

*Follow Up, Follow
Through, and Stay in Touch*

Tanya, who sells copy machines for a national firm, called her client, Frank, the head of facilities for Texas corporate headquarters. She made it a standard practice to either call or e-mail Frank once per month to check in. While on the phone Frank thanked her for the golf tips she sent on "how to shave five strokes off your game." In closing he told her to call Kevin, a colleague who runs the facility for them in Decatur. She flipped open her laptop , captured Kevin's contact information, and will now be able to let Frank know when she schedules the appointment.

The days of jotting down the name of a referral on a loose piece of paper or storing everything in your head about a previous conversation are over. You need one place to keep track of what was said and what actions are required.

Being organized is critical to the success of *SuperNetworking*. Tanya made it seem so easy. It's not! This is where most sales professionals fall short. It is critical to the success of this program. Your efficiency and effectiveness will be greatly enhanced by your ability to build and maintain a personal network database.

The importance of developing and maintaining a database of your network of contacts cannot be over-emphasized. And not just for selling more and making more money, but for life in general. When your plan is fully launched, you will be at the early stages of building a strong network. Over time, the contacts you make and information you gain will improve your quality of life. I have made countless friends through my network, and I could fill up the rest of the book with stories about how certain people have made a big difference in my life. The best example I gave you was in Chapter 3 when I explained how I met my wife. If you remember she (the referral) first "blew me off." However, because I had to follow up and go back to see her roommate (my contact) to retrieve my grill, I was able to keep the process moving forward, and the rest, as they say, is history.

Being able to get an appointment with the best heart surgeon at Massachusetts General Hospital when he is telling others that he is not taking any new patients, or having a contact to get you a reservation at the "hottest" restaurant in town, is a simple example of how life will be when you constantly maintain and access your network of contacts.

It is up to you to drive this process. The strength and size of your network are going to be a reflection of the amount of time and effort you put into it. By keeping track of your network of personal contacts, you will be in control of managing your business, which will give you the confidence to make this a positive experience.

Keeping Track of Your Progress

It is important that you set up specific fields in your *SuperNetworking* database so you can easily access your data. This will save you time when an important phone call comes in or when you are looking at who you should call back on what particular day.

Your efficiency will be greatly enhanced by investing in your personal network database. But, as with a bank account, if you do not put anything in, you won't get anything out. If you don't keep track of your progress here and you let things slip through the cracks, you are not going to get as much out of this program as you should. You must take the time to capture all the information in one place in order to improve your efficiency and effectiveness. As I mentioned in Chapter 3, you can use software packages such as ACT, Gold Mine, or Sales Logix, or you can even keep the information in an Excel spreadsheet.

Critical Database Information

The key fields of information to capture in every phone call are listed here. Some of the fields were discussed in Chapter 3 when you put your initial contact list together. Now that the process is moving forward, you will have contacts and referrals to call and you'll need to add some more fields and organize your database in a way that makes it easy for you to manage the process.

This database structure has been designed to help you stay focused on what is truly important and eliminate the minutia. The critical fields are:

- ◆ **Contact name.** This is the person you are calling.
- ◆ **Title (if known).** Mr./Ms./Mrs./Dr. If you have this information before your call, great.

If not, it would help if you ask during the conversation.

- **Company name.** Make sure you have the correct spelling.

- **Phone number.** Again, attention to this type of detail is very important.

- **E-mail address.** Many things can go wrong here. In order to make sure you captured this information correctly, repeat it to your contact.

- **Referred by.** This would be the person who told you to call. This is your door-opener for a warm call.

- **Date of contact.** Enter the date for every communication you have.

- **Date for follow-up.** As discussed throughout *SuperNetworking*, every call should lead to some future activity. This will help you keep track of when you have to execute an activity on a specific day.

- **Status.** This will give you a quick synopsis of where things stand with this individual.

- **Action.** This will let you know what is supposed to happen next.

- **Thank-you note sent.** As stated earlier, people like to be asked and thanked. Let them you know you appreciate what they have done or will be doing for you in the future.

- **Comments.** Here is where you can put additional information that did not fit into the other fields. You may learn something in your initial conversation that will have relevance in the future, such as interests, hobbies, and

personal information, such as family information. Capture that information here.

Follow Up and Follow Through

The way you follow up and follow through after each
call is extremely important. Most conversations with a
contact will trigger some type of action on your part. You
may have been asked to submit a proposal or to follow up
with e-mail. Because your actions speak louder than words,
always do what you said you were going to do in a timely
manner. Following are some scenarios that are likely to
occur and how you should follow up on them.

The Referral Gave You the Names of Some Other People to Call

Be sure that you understand exactly how the referral
would like to handle this. Will the referral be calling ahead
to introduce you, or are you supposed to call and mention
the referral's name? Either way, make a note in your planner to call your new contact when you agreed you would.

The Referral Is Scheduling a Meeting for You

Agree on a date and time during the call, and immediately record it in your planner.

As you follow up, you need to remain organized and
learn to prioritize your activities. You must always live up
to your commitments. Stay focused, and don't let anything
or anyone get in the way of what you need to do. Remember that your referrals will be judging you on how you
follow up and conduct yourself.

Don't get busy with new activities and let existing commitments slide, as this will create a negative impression
that this will make on other people. Your credibility is on

the line here, and you must execute effectively. Mrs. Fields (the cookie mogul) says, "Good enough never is." Don't just meet expectations; exceed them.

Ways to Stay in Touch

There are so many ways to follow through by staying in touch or showing your appreciation to your contacts and referrals. Here are a few suggestions to keep the lines of communication strong:

- **Phone calls.** Keep your client, contact, or referral in the loop as things progress, especially any developments with the people to whom he introduced you. He may hear of something else or can give you insight on how best to proceed to bring the sales process forward or help you close the deal.

- **E-mail.** This is the same as the follow-up phone call. Keep all e-mails short and simple.

- **Thank-you note or blank card by mail.** Not many people send cards anymore. How many did you receive in the last 12 months? Exactly! This is another way to separate you from your peers. People remember and appreciate them.

- **Send an article.** If you know that people have interests in certain subjects, and you see an interesting article on such topics, send it along. It shows that you are a good listener and you have a good memory. I recently sent an article from *The New York Times* about Curt Schilling of the Boston Red Sox to a client who is also a die-hard Sox fan. It was well received and very much appreciated.

- **Offer your help.** Offer to reciprocate by asking if there's anything you can do for him. For example, maybe he is planning to buy a car, and you have a contact at a dealership. Maybe he needs some help painting a room in his house. Give-and-take will go a long way.

- **Become a referral.** Perhaps you can introduce your contact to someone who can help her. Now you are becoming a resource for others. I called a good friend of mine and spoke to his secretary. In conversation I learned that her son was looking to become an editor for a publishing house in Boston. I offered to introduce her son to my public relations firm contact and agent, who know many people in that field. She took me up on the offer, her son got interviews, and eventually he received several offers, which came through the referrals I gave her. That's another example of the power of *SuperNetworking*.

- **Personal updates.** Let people know what's happening in your personal life (graduations, weddings, and so forth). This humanizes you and lets people see you in a different light.

- **Invitations.** Invite a contact to a ball game, movie, or dinner. It's another way of saying thank you, and it gives you a chance to spend some time with him and enhance the relationship.

- **Recreational activities.** Invite your contacts to go fishing, play golf, or go for a run.

- **Send holiday cards.** In addition to the traditional holidays, you can stand out from the crowd by sending a card on the occasion of another holiday. Include a warm note, a thank you note, or a personal update.

How Often You Stay in Touch

This really depends on the type of relationship you have with certain individuals and what their preferences may be. You certainly don't want to contact people too often and be perceived as either pushy or a nuisance. On the other hand, you don't want to be invisible so that, when you do call, people refer to you as "stranger." And you don't want to be perceived as a person who only calls when he needs something. Remember: Networking is a two-way street. It's about giving and receiving. In order to keep the lines of communication open, you should follow a plan so that it becomes a habit.

Stay-in-Touch Form

		How Often to Stay in Touch					
		Weekly	Monthly	Bimonthly	Quarterly	Biannually	Annually
Contacts	A	X	X				
	B		X	X			
	C			X	X		
	D				X	X	X

How about we just do a quick recap? If you read the entire chapter you now know:

- ◆ How to keep track of your progress to keep your network strong so things do not "slip through the cracks."
- ◆ The critical data fields to enter into your database.
- ◆ The value and importance of strong follow-up and follow-through.
- ◆ Ways to stay in touch with your network of contacts to keep the lines of communication strong.
- ◆ How often to stay in touch with your network of contacts to keep the lines of communication open.

Chapter 8

Report to Your Mentor:

Formalize the Process and Stay Focused

Claudia, a sole practitioner, sells handbags to retail stores. She was always busy and thought she was doing well. She sat down with her mentor, Giselle, and said, "I was so busy last week, what an improvement from the week before." Giselle pointed out that she was not staying on task. She was having enjoyable chats but her sales revenue was not increasing, the number of new contacts was in the unacceptable range, and the number of new proposals submitted was zero. It was very sobering for Claudia to see her results in black and white. The next week she stuck to her plan, prepared for and made the necessary calls, and hadn't forgotten the action items. Now she showed real improvement! These formal weekly meetings with Giselle kept her focused on what was truly important.

Everyone needs someone to be accountable when they are responsible for driving revenue for an organization, whether you are an owner, manager, sole practitioner, or salesperson. Realistically, once you start executing your plan, you are going to get very busy and will need some help to keep track of your progress. In order for this *SuperNetworking* plan to succeed, you must find a mentor to whom you can report and meet with formally on a weekly basis. This mentor will serve as your boss and hold you accountable to qualitative and quantitative measures. At the end of this chapter, you will go through a mentor selection criteria checklist to show you how to select the right person for you.

Why Is it Important to Have a Mentor?

If your boss told you that he needed a project completed by 5 p.m. tomorrow, no questions asked, there is a 99.9-percent chance that you will deliver on time. Now if you are in a small business, an owner, your own boss, run a practice, or sole practitioner, chances are 50 percent you will complete the task on time. That's just human nature. You'll rationalize it and probably tell yourself, "I think I'll finish it tomorrow." Right? Having a mentor will force you to live up to your commitments and exceed even your own expectations.

A mentor helps formalize the process. Once the plan goes into effect, you will become busy with sending out e-mails, phone calls, meetings, submitting proposals, and follow-up. Things can start to get lost in any number of ways and you risk losing credibility with prospective clients. This is where most sales professionals fail, struggle, or are criticized for. So many people start out with good intentions, but over time you can get distracted or start rationalizing and wind up saying, "I'll go back on it tomorrow." In sales you say, "I'll just get to it tomorrow." But tomorrow never happens, and people do not stay on course. They miss an opportunity (maybe even "the one" that can make their years) and damage their reputations along the way. A mentor will keep you on track. For the sales professionals who currently have a boss and meet formally on a regular basis, you are all set. For the small business person, owner, your own boss, sole practitioner, or anyone else who has responsibility generating revenue for an organization, having a mentor gives this part of the *SuperNetworking* process the structure and discipline required to help you stay on course.

Claudia thought she was doing a great job until she sat down with Giselle, her mentor. Giselle gave her another perspective that Claudia needed in order to improve her performance. A good mentor will formalize the process, hold you accountable to set standards, increase your productivity, improve your efficiency and effectiveness, keep you focused only on revenue-producing activities that effect the top and bottom line, and impact the amount of money put into your pocket. That's truly what Claudia wanted out of the relationship. Isn't that what you want, too?

What Will a Mentor Do for Me?

A mentor will give you objectivity and help you make intelligent, informed decisions. A mentor will serve as a sounding board for you. You may come up with what appears to be a good sales strategy and call objective for a crucial meeting. A mentor will let you know if it makes sense, is reality-based, and has a good chance for success. A mentor will help you crystallize your thoughts and give you additional ideas to consider. A mentor will help give you the substance and confidence you need.

The sales business gives you tremendous highs and lows. When things are hectic and you are constantly on the phone, going to meetings, submitting proposals, and making new connections, you feel great. When things are not going as well as you planned and you have doubt whether you can hit your quota, a sense of panic can set in. Having a mentor work with you will give you stability in what is often a roller-coaster ride of emotions. Here are some important things a mentor will do for you:

- Give you the objectivity you need to make good and informed decisions.
- Formalize the process and help you stay focused on revenue-producing activities.
- Encourage you to work your plan consistently to maximize your opportunities.
- Be honest with you and hold you accountable when your performance is falling short.
- Give you words of encouragement and pump you up when you need it.
- Keep you levelheaded in good times and bad.

Part of a mentor's role is qualitative as well as quantitative. A mentor should also be available to help you with issues at all stages of your process, whether it is developing sales strategies, call objectives, or your elevator pitch or constructing phone scripts.

Your mentor will keep you on your toes. A good mentor will provide positive reinforcement but also apply appropriate pressure when needed. Maintaining that sort of balance is very important throughout the process.

What Will a Mentor Expect From Me?

Even if you have either a personal or professional connection with this person, do not forget what role she serves in this process. For the sales professionals who currently have a manager, you understand that your mentor is your boss and treat them as such. For people who work in businesses that do not have a sales manager (business owners, sole practitioners, and so forth) you need to treat this person as if she *is* your manager. She will treat this relationship professionally and you should, too.

Your mentor will have certain expectations. Here is what you need to do to keep your mentor engaged in this process:

- **Show weekly progress.** During your scheduled weekly meeting, be prepared to discuss the qualitative and quantitative aspects of your progress.
- **Display honesty.** Tell the truth to your mentor. It's the best way he or she can help you.
- **Live up to your commitments.** Deliver on your promises. Remember: This person is doing you a favor. Do what you say you are going to, and don't make excuses.
- **Put forth a "herculean" effort.** This plan is hard work. Don't cheat yourself or your mentor.
- **Focus.** You can easily get distracted. Stay the course you set out with your mentor, and do not deviate from the plan unless you mutually agree to specific change.
- **Don't waste your mentor's time.** Nothing more needs to be said.

158 • SuperNetworking for Sales Pros

What's in it for the Mentor?

The right mentors want you to have as much success and prosperity as possible. They care about doing what they can do to contribute to your professional success and financial well-being. Sales managers generally get compensated based on a percentage of what you bring in. As your mentor and manager, he already has an incentive to keep you on the straight and narrow. A mentor who is not your direct supervisor will not be looking for a monetary award. He will be happy for you and feel good about his role in your success. He will likely think back to when other people helped him in his life. Here is what a mentor wants. (If your mentor is looking for anything else, you have the wrong person.)

- Satisfaction from having an impact.
- Recognition.
- Acknowledgment.
- Appreciation.

How Do I Ask Someone to Be My Mentor?

For the sales professionals who currently have a boss this should be easy. You are just asking them to evaluate your performance with an additional optic. For the rest of us it may appear to be a difficult task, but it really shouldn't be. You will be asking someone you know and trust to help you out. And laying out the rules right from the start will guide both of you toward success.

Once you identify the right person, follow the outline and script, and you will have a commitment from your mentor. The right person for you is out there. You just have to ask.

Elements of a Successful Script
When You Do Not Have a Boss

1. Value her time.
2. Explain the situation.
3. Express that you value her time and opinion.
4. Ask for help.
5. Describe the mentoring process.
6. Ask for a commitment.

Script: Asking for a Mentor Script When You Do Not Have a Boss

1. Value her time.

Dan: Rebecca. Hi, it's Dan. Do you have a minute?

Rebecca: Sure. What's up?

2. Explain the situation.

Dan: As you know I am responsible for new sales with my company. As part of my approach I am looking for someone to support me, essentially as a coach as I go through this process.

Rebecca: Sounds interesting. Conceptually it makes sense.

Express that you value her time and opinion.

Dan: I think you know how important our association is. I respect and value your opinion. It really means a lot to me.

Rebecca: Thanks. The feeling is mutual.

4. Ask for help.

Dan: I would like to talk to you about being my mentor in this process.

Rebecca: Really? Before I make any commitment, what would I need to do?

5. Describe the mentoring process.

Dan: In essence, you would be my boss. We would formally get together once a week and we would review my progress. There are weekly progress forms I would submit to you, and we would be discussing my results in a quantitative and qualitative way. No different than if you were my sales manager.

6. Ask for a commitment.

Dan: So what do you think?

Rebecca: Sounds okay so far.

Elements of a Successful Script When You Have a Boss

1. Value her time.
2. Explain the situation.
3. Describe the mentoring process.
4. Ask for a commitment.

Script: Asking for a Mentor When You Already Have a Boss

1. Value her time.

Sid: Sue, do you have a minute?

Sue: Yes. What can I do for you?

2. Explain the situation.

Sid: I am undertaking a program that I really think will drastically improve my production. Part of the methodology is that I need to select a mentor, a coach in the process who will make sure I live up to commitments and hit certain milestones. It really would be an extension of some of the things we cover during our weekly meetings.

Rebecca: Sounds interesting. Tell me more.

3. Describe the mentoring process.

Sid: We would continue to meet formally one day a week, and we would review my progress on my *SuperNetworking*) initiatives. There are weekly progress forms I would submit to you and we would be discussing my results in a quantitative and qualitative way. No different than what we do now, just using an additional measurement criterion to specifically track my networking initiatives and the results from my efforts including actual revenues.

4. Ask for a commitment.

Sid: So what do you think?

Sue: Anything that will help produce more revenue for the company is a good thing. Let's do it.

Criteria for Selecting a Mentor

Obviously if you have a sales manager as a boss, you will more than likely choose your boss as your mentor. However, if you don't, you need to think about who in your life might be a good mentor. There are certain criteria to look for. Here are the essential ingredients:

- ◆ Trust.
- ◆ Honesty.
- ◆ Candor.
- ◆ Reliability.
- ◆ Demanding and willing to push you.
- ◆ Objectivity.
- ◆ High standards.
- ◆ Will not let you off the hook.

Who Should I Consider Choosing?

Now that you have identified the qualities of a good mentor, you need to start thinking about the right person for you.

There are people in your life who you may be close to but who would not be the right mentor. One example is your significant other. This person certainly has an enormous interest in your being successful but will probably not be as objective as you would like, and this can frequently lead to an uncomfortable situation. Earning a livelihood is serious business, and the relationship with your mentor should be as well.

Here are some suggestions for people that you may want to consider:

- ◆ **Former bosses.** They know you and probably know of what you are capable. They have been your boss before and know how to motivate you.

- ◆ **Business partner.** They certainly have a vested interest in your success. Also, who in business knows you better? Just knowing you have to meet with this person formally once a week and look him in the eye to report on your performance is a great motivator.

- ◆ **Former colleague.** They also know of what you are capable and can provide solid advice and speak to you "as if they are in your shoes."

- ◆ **Siblings or relatives.** They are your family, and family members generally have an unwavering commitment to you, win, lose, or draw. Their senses of loyalty and commitment to you and the process will be very strong.

- ◆ **Close friends.** Just as siblings or relatives, they have the same motivation to help you. My mentor is a close friend. I attribute part of my success to his involvement. His intelligence, wisdom, temperament, instincts, interest, and contribution have been a huge part of the process. I truly look forward to seeing him every week. It's a great reason to get together and in some ways has brought us closer.

Who Shouldn't I Choose?

There might be people in your life who appear to be candidates to be your mentor, but, after you conduct a thorough diagnostic, you realize they are not the best people for you. Here are some people that you should avoid and why:

- ◆ **Spouses.** Some people would select this person for the obvious reason: Your spouse has a vested interest and is very accessible. This is the person with whom you confide in the most and probably knows you better than anyone else. The danger/problem is that your spouse is too close. If you have a spouse you probably understand this point. If you don't, trust me on this one!

- **Anyone expecting a monetary award.** If someone asks you, "What will you pay me for my time?" or "What percentage will you give me from your commissions?" you have the wrong person.

- **Anyone too close to you.** On the surface close friends might appear to be good candidates to be your mentor, but this may not be the case. This relationship requires total candor, and every relationship you have with close friends is different. Despite your closeness you might not be comfortable discussing certain things with them, or feel you don't want them to know this part of your life.

- **Yourself.** You cannot be your own mentor. You need someone who is objective, and you can't be. Period.

- **No one.** As with choosing yourself, this plan will fail if you do not choose someone to be your mentor.

Chapter 9

Embrace Accountability:

Track Your Progress and Measure Results

Dave's confidence was sky high. A sales executive for an electronics distributor, he regularly exceeded his quota, received referrals constantly, and hadn't needed to make a cold call in 12 months. His phone was ringing off the hook with people looking to help him. Abby, his sales manager, wanted to know what was going on. Dave grinned and said, "Once you set those exceptional levels for me to reach and kept me on my *SuperNetworking* plan, I knew I could do it." Great Daves are created when there's a powerful accountability system.

> "If you cannot measure it, you cannot manage it."
> —Paul Kazarian, Investment Banking Professional

I am sure you have heard the expression "sales is a numbers game." I agree. Over time, the numbers always bear this out. A sales profeesional's goal is generally defined as his or her quota. If you only focus on your end result and do not understand what it takes to get you there, you will generally fail. Missing a quota is a recipe for termination. Exceeding a quota is your ticket for advancement and for more money in your pocket. If your pipeline is dry, you will have a difficult time making quota. If you have lots of activity in the pipeline, chances are you will exceed your quota. Stay focused on the process. Do it every day, keep your funnel full of meaningful *SuperNetworking* activity, and the results will take care of themselves and great things will happen for you.

I stated at the beginning that this is hard work. There are no shortcuts to success, and building a *SuperNetwork* takes time and effort. The people who think that it is too tough are the ones who will rationalize why they did not reach their numbers. The individuals who constantly exceed the weekly expectations will be in the money sooner than they ever expected. You make the choice.

Weekly Progress Report: Your Mentor Wants Your Numbers

Accountability and responsibility are essential elements that guarantee you have more and better-qualified leads. Before each regularly scheduled meeting with your mentor, you will be responsible for a weekly report that tracks your progress and provides a reality check on where you are relative to your goals and objectives. The information in your database will be used as a reference point when you work with your mentor during the *qualitative* portion of your weekly discussions.

Your database will also help you in preparing for the *quantitative* portion of your weekly meeting. These are specific numbers-based performance standards with clear benchmarks of critical success factors. These are numbers you need to reach every week. Your mentor will hold you accountable to these measurements.

The uniqueness of the *SuperNetworking* program is the combination of having a mentor and having a numbers-based system with set standards to track your progress and results. By achieving these specific numbers-based standards every week, you *will* see immediate results.

Having to present documentation that reports your progress might bring back memories. Whether it was bringing home your report card or meeting with your boss on a weekly basis, we have all been in these situations. You have to show someone what you have done, and it's much more powerful if it's there in black and white. It can be pretty sobering, but it will help push you. You won't want to be embarrassed by submitting a less-than-favorable report card on yourself, especially when you have so much to gain or lose.

Ed Koch, former mayor of New York, used to go around the city and ask people, "How am I doing?" Well, this is the documentation that lets you and your mentor know exactly how you are doing.

The standards of performance and critical success factors set forth are based on time-tested results. They will give you a return on investment (ROI), which will be your payoff from all your hard work. I've created a form that you can use (on page 172–173) to measure these standards of performance.

Standards of Performance

◆ **Unacceptable performance.** If your weekly numbers are consistently at an unacceptable level, it will be much harder to be successful and exceed revenue projections. That's a fact.

- ◆ **Acceptable performance.** These are the bare minimum numbers you should achieve. If you are consistently on the high end, you will find yourself busy and getting closer to reaching your sales objective.

- ◆ **Exceptional performance.** If you are reaching these numbers, you will make a lot of money. You will probably land more business than ever before and more money than you thought possible. I would love to see the look on your face when you are staring at the numbers on your W-2 or bank statement.

Critical Success Factors

- ◆ **Number of networking calls made.** It all starts with making the initial client or contact call to get this process rolling. You have developed names from the initial contact list. When you start talking to more people, you will start making more connections, which will open up more doors for you. If you are using the scripts properly, you should have plenty of calls to make.

- ◆ **Number of new networking contacts established.** We've learned that, as you peel the onion, you should get additional referrals. You will have enough people in your contact list to make many warm calls and get you closer to the right person.

- ◆ **Number of meetings scheduled.** If you are scheduling meetings, you are getting closer to your goal. In order to have the possibility of success you must put yourself in a position to succeed.

- ◆ **Number of proposals submitted.** The actual number of proposals may not be a fair representation, because one large sale could be bigger than 10 little sales. However, I do know that, if you are not generating enough quality proposals, you will never get to your ultimate goal.

- ◆ **Number of proposals awarded and/or number of new clients.** The actual number here is also deceptive for the same reason previously mentioned. However, if you are getting more and better qualified opportunities through leveraging your network of contacts, and most things are equal relative to price, product, and service, chances are if your request for a proposal came by way of your network, you'll get the sale.

- ◆ **$ Amount expected from your network per month.** This number will vary depending on a variety of circumstances. However, this should become the byproduct of all of the other metrics listed here.

You know what your objectives are. I can't set them for you. This is something you need to do for yourself or with your mentor. We are on the honor system here. Stretch yourself with fair and reasonable goals. Listed on page 172–173 is the Accountability and Responsibility Form, which provides a place for you to enter your projected and actual numbers. Use this form as your weekly progress report and present it to your mentor at your weekly sessions.

Forecast

These are the numbers that you will be measured against and for which you will be held accountable. Notice that the "$ Amount Expected from Your Network per

Month" field is blank. The reason is because you need to stay focused on the five other fields on a daily basis and reach exceptional levels on a weekly and monthly basis. These are the activities that will drive your process. If you stay committed to achieving exceptional numbers, the offers will follow.

Actual

These are the actual numbers you will enter on a weekly basis to be used when meeting with your mentor. You are on the honor system here. If you inflate your numbers, you are only kidding yourself. This information can be easily taken from the information entered in your database.

I recently conducted a workshop for a region of one of the country's largest privately held facilities management firms. We put 30 account managers through the program. These people were not directly responsible for sales. However, in their capacities they have the ability to identify additional sales opportunities for the organization. It was agreed that I would serve as the group's mentor, conduct monthly phone meetings, and meet face to face on a quarterly basis. The regional vice president, John, told me that, if his group could bring an additional $1.3MM in revenue from networking over the next 12 months, he would be more than happy.

During the first quarterly regional meeting we spent a good portion of time talking about refining elevator and sales pitches. We also allocated an hour to review the progress reports. As we began discussing the results there was a sense of apprehension. Remember when your parents asked you to come see them and you thought you were in trouble? That was the feeling they had. Because these managers came from all over the region nobody really knew how the others were doing according to the forecasted objectives. Overall, the numbers of the actual networking calls bordered on the unacceptable to the acceptable range.

The number of new contacts was in the acceptable level range. The number of meetings scheduled and proposals submitted bordered on acceptable to exceptional. The actual number of proposals won and actual dollar amount exceeded the exceptional forecast for the entire year. When we were done totaling things up, the group had generated $1.5MM in one quarter.

Needless to say the mood changed, with everyone breathing easier and smiles all around. After a few jokes and kudos all around, I asked the group to take a step back to look at the numbers and trends. What they learned was that, once they got an opportunity, their "hit ratio" was outstanding. They also realized that, if they increased their level of activity by increasing their number of initial calls and new contacts established, they could have greater success, more revenue for the region, more opportunities for them and others, and more money in their pockets. They left the room more committed than ever to do better next quarter. As I write this book we are in the early stages of their second quarter, so I can't give you additional results. However, what was interesting was seeing their reactions when they were reviewing their activities in black and white. You could feel their confidence level rise as the numbers grew. By formalizing the process they were held accountable to a standard of performance they never would have achieved without utilizing this progress report.

If a group of account managers who does not have day-to-day responsibility for sales can produce the way it did by following the *SuperNetworking* process, you can, too. Just stay focused on the process and consistently exceed your weekly objectives, and great things will happen for you, just as it did the account managers.

ACCOUNTABILITY AND RESPONSIBILITY—WEEKLY PROGRESS REPORT FOR LEVERAGING AND INCREASING PERSONAL & PROFESSIONAL NETWORK					
	# of Calls Per Week	# of New Contacts Established Per Week	# of Meetings Per Week	# of Proposals Submitted Per Month	# of New Clients Per Month	$ Amount Expected from Network Per Month
UNACCEPTABLE						
ACCEPTABLE						
EXCEPTIONAL						

ACCOUNTABILITY AND RESPONSIBILITY—WEEKLY PROGRESS REPORT FOR LEVERAGING AND INCREASING PERSONAL & PROFESSIONAL NETWORK						
	# of Calls	# of New Contacts Established	# of Meetings Scheduled	# of Proposals Submitted	# of New Clients	$ Amount Expected from Network
WEEK 1						
WEEK 2						
WEEK 3						
WEEK 4						
WEEK 5						
WEEK 6						
WEEK 7						
WEEK 8						

Chapter 10

Enjoy Your Future:

Create a Network for Life

Perry was giddy with excitement. He was looking at the database of contacts he had developed over the past 24 months. He realized that, if he hadn't leveraged his network of contacts the way he had, then he wouldn't be about to buy that new, dark green BMW X5. As he was reflecting, he received a call from a good friend, Susan, one of the many people who had helped him. In conversation, he learned that Susan's son was graduating from high school and had selected Boston College as college of his choice. Perry knew people at the school and offered to see if he could help. Susan took Perry up on his offer, and her son was, in fact, admitted. Perry felt just as good about helping Susan's son as he did about the new car. Perry understood that networking is a two-way street, and in life it's all about who you know, not so much what you know.

You've made it. The time and effort you've put forth in following this program has paid off. When you started out, you were not quite sure if you had it in you to stay the course, but you did, and now you realize just how much better off you are.

You have not only changed the way you approach your business, but also how you approach your life. The majority of people have heard the word *networking*, and you now understand it conceptually. More importantly you now know the "how to." Here's what you have accomplished. You have:

- ◆ Learned how to determine your value proposition in a way that highlights your professional strengths and your company's competitive advantages.

- ◆ Developed an effective elevator pitch that is narrowly focused and captures your target audience's attention, providing them with precisely what they need to know in order to help you. And, you can now articulate your value proposition in a clear and concise manner.

- ◆ Learned the importance of having an overall networking sales strategy, from a macro level leading to a focus on target profile accounts making it easy for people to help you.

- ◆ Learned the importance of having a call strategy and call objective for every networking opportunity or initiative, ensuring you reach the desired outcome for every conversation you have.

- ◆ Organized and categorized your network of contacts appropriately so that you know who and why you want to call.

- ◆ Learned how to "peel the onion" until you get to the core—that is, to the right person who can help you.

- ◆ Learned the value of preparing for each phone call to make a favorable impression on everyone with whom you speak and earn credibility (which is the most long-lasting and permanent type) with your referrals.

- ◆ Learned the do's and don'ts of how to conduct yourself in any networking endeavor to ensure that you always make a favorable first impression.

- ◆ Developed effective scripts that make it easy to ask people to help, extract promises ensuring the outcome you desire, and receive more qualified leads.

- ◆ Learned the importance of follow-up and follow-through by building and maintaining a network database, ensuring that things do not "slip through the cracks."

- ◆ Learned ways to stay in touch to keep the lines of communication open and the network strong.

- ◆ Learned how to find and use a mentor who is able to help you formalize the process and keep you focused.

- ◆ Learned how to prepare a weekly performance report that your mentor is able to use to monitor your progress, hold you accountable, and measure your return on investment.

- ◆ Learned how to develop more relationships and expand your network of contacts.

- ◆ Learned how to maximize business opportunities, increase your base of business, generate

more revenue for your company, and make
more money for yourself.

◆ Learned how to maintain a *SuperNetwork* for
life.

The Art of *SuperNetworking*

Generating more revenue for your company and making more money for yourself was just a byproduct of the
work you did and the new skills you developed. The art
of *SuperNetworking* is a life skill that will change the way
you function in the world. You are now better equipped
to handle many challenges as your world continues to
change. *SuperNetworking* is about building relationships—
for life.

It is important to keep your network fresh and up to
date throughout your life. If you do, you will be able to
accomplish anything you want professionally or personally. Your life will become much easier. Every now and then
you need a reminder of how powerful your *SuperNetwork*
can be. Here's an example of a time-sensitive situation
that happened to me. My COBRA health insurance ex-
pired, and I was having trouble with a particular health
insurance carrier. I thought I would just call a few other
carriers, compare quotes, select the best one, and be done
with it. I was wrong. I learned that I was going to wait an
inordinate amount of time to get the coverage I wanted.
Needless to say, I was agitated. Rather than spend countless hours trying to find a better carrier, I took a step back
and thought about whom in my network I could call to
help. I made one call to a client and friend, John Carew, a
partner in New England's largest and fastest-growing independent benefits brokerage agency. I explained the situation in less than five minutes. John told me to sit tight.
He was going to make a phone call and would have a

contact name for me within 30 minutes. John called back five minutes later and suggested I call Mike McCarthy and use his name. I called Mike. The same day he sent me plan options. The next day I signed up, and within two weeks I had coverage.

Taking what could have been a stressful situation and diffusing it in a matter of minutes was invaluable to me. Making the call to John was the best thing I could have done. Just talking to him and having him tell me not to worry and that he could help made me feel so much better. The referral, Mike, couldn't have been any nicer and made the transition seamless. Do you think I would have received the same treatment if I had gotten to Mike on a cold call? I seriously doubt I would have ever gotten to him, let alone know that he was the "right person." Utilizing my network saved me time and energy and made my life so much easier. I am grateful to John for what he did for me and offered to return the favor.

What do you think will happen if you don't maintain your network? Think about the difference between you and someone else whose network is larger and stronger. Their ability to access people or information at a moment's notice allows them to be more efficient and effective than you. Think of the time saved by knowing how to get results quickly because you've made valuable connections for life.

I suppose you can think of the following story as an example of "practicing what I preach." When I decided to write my first book, *SuperNetworking: Reach the Right People, Build Your Career Network, and Land Your Dream Job—Now,* I felt there might be a business opportunity, too. I wanted to create a networking methodology company and teach people in a workshop the same skills that you have developed in this book. I wanted a course curriculum that could be delivered in a classroom environment. I studied the training business and researched other networking experts. At the time I didn't know much about the training business. My instincts told me to look at my network of contacts to see who would be able to help. My first call went to David, a contact and friend who used to work for a technical training company. His insight into the business was invaluable. I also called another contact, Gerry, who helped me put my first book proposal together. Gerry liked my idea and put me in touch with his friend, Stacy, who used to be the head of instructional design for Accenture, who was experienced in developing workshop curriculum. The input I received from David and Stacy helped shape my business model. I had numerous phone calls, lunches, and dinners with both of them over the course of the next six months, and they wanted nothing in return. They just wanted to help.

David referred me to Beran, who became a great resource. Beran referred me to a great graphic designer who developed my brochure and an outstanding Web design firm that built my Website. Again, having these contacts saved me a tremendous amount of time and made my life so much easier. I am grateful for the opportunity to work with these people, and I could never have accomplished these tasks without doing my own *SuperNetworking*.

By accessing my network of contacts, I was able to meet some very talented people who are now in my database permanently. I now know where to go when I need help in specific areas. This saved me a tremendous amount of time. Also, it feels great working with people you know and/or who come through a referral. There is an additional element of trust and confidence that gives you peace of mind. Whether it is taking your car in for repair, picking out a diamond for your significant other, or finding the best daycare for your children, you simply feel better when an introduction comes from network of contacts.

These contacts, Stacy and Beran, who were originally referrals, have introduced me to other people who have also helped me in many ways. Besides having a professional relationship with some of these people, a personal relationship has developed too. I play golf with David and socialize with Stacy. I attribute my successful relationships to the amount of time I put into developing and maintaining my network of contacts. That is the payoff of having a strong *SuperNetwork*. You just have to make it a priority. Don't wait until it is too late. Get in the habit now.

Giving and Receiving Is a 2-Way Street

At the beginning of this process, you were the beneficiary of help from others. Now that you are an experienced networker, it is very important that you remember what others have done to help you attain success. You are now in a position to return the favor and help others when they are doing their own networking. If a particular event or occurrence makes you think of someone in your network, try to think of a way you can help him or her either personally or professionally. It does not have to be to "return the favor" or for a specific purpose. If you are always asking and never give back, your network will become weak and inefficient. You will be viewed as a "taker," not a "giver." Do not let this happen to you.

A friend of mine and contact, John Lander, is also a member of my board of advisors. John started out as a referral. He and I were introduced by Bob Devlin. John is what I consider a center of influence (COI). If I need tickets to a game or a reservation at one of Boston's top restaurants, John is my guy. A friendship has evolved over the past few years. We play golf together and socialize as couples, and his friendship and guidance in my business has been invaluable. John has helped me in many different ways, and I have regularly asked him what I might do to help him, because it was my desire to demonstrate my appreciation for all he has done for me. He said, "I just want to see you become successful and I will help you in any way possible." John was not looking for anything in return. This is how your network should work if it is to be optimally effective.

Because John is on my A list, I speak to him on a regular basis, at least two to three times per month. These discussions provide both of us the opportunity to inform each other about what is happening in our respective personal and professional lives. John called me recently to let me know that he has, for the first time, become a grandfather. His daughter, Stephanie, is now the mother of twin daughters. I obtained Stephanie's home address and sent a gift. This was another example of a way for me to recognize John and express my appreciation to him. This is a perfect example of how a network should operate.

John and his actuarial staff at Lander & Associates have been life insurance product innovators for more than 25 years. In response to recent tax law changes they have designed a life insurance arrangement that appears to me to be the most cost-efficient method for high-net-worth individuals to transfer assets to children, grandchildren, and charity. During one of our conversations, John explained his firm's new product offering and described the product's target audience. I mentioned to John that I had a good lifelong friend who is an estate-planning and tax attorney and represents the type of people John would like to know. I scheduled a dinner for the two of them to meet, and they got along famously. The strength of both of my network's relationships opened a door for each person that would have never happened had I not been thinking about helping my network partners. These are the type of things that happen when you are involved in *SuperNetworking*.

Do not wait for someone to do you a favor before you do something for them. Be an initiator, not a reactor! If you step back from the hectic nature of everyday life and allow yourself a few minutes to reflect on those people who are in your network, you will very easily arrive at something you can do for each person. In many cases, it can simply be regular telephone calls to stay in touch and learn how he, his family, and/or his business is doing. Everyone desires to feel wanted and important. You have the power, within you, to make someone feel special. Take charge. There are many creative ways to show your appreciation for the people in your network. It sends a strong message that you really care about them. In return, people will be much more likely to help you when it is you who are asking for a favor (quid pro quo).

Here is an important point for you to know. Don't feel uncomfortable asking people for help even if you haven't done something for them first. This is natural. There are situations where you get to help people before they have a chance to reciprocate, and other times it's the reverse. *SuperNetworking* is based on contacts, not timing. In the long run things will even out. But be conscious if relationships become one-sided, and adjust your approach and scripts appropriately.

Robert B. Cialdini, a professor at Arizona State, wrote a book, *Influence: Science and Practice*. One of the chapters was dedicated to reciprocation. In it he writes:

> *According to sociologists and anthropologists, one*
> *of the most widespread and basic norms of human*

culture is embodied in the rule of reciprocation. The rule requires that one person try to repay, in kind, what another person has provided. This sense of future obligation within the rules makes possible the development of various kinds of continuing relationships, transactions, and exchanges that are beneficial to the society. Consequently, all members of society are trained from childhood to abide by the rule or suffer serious social disapproval.

One favorite tactic of certain compliance professionals is to give something back before asking for a favor. The rule can spur uneven exchanges: to be rid of the uncomfortable feeling of indebtedness, an individual will often agree to a request for a substantially larger favor than the one he or she received.

That is not how *SuperNetworking* works. If your contacts or referrals have their "hand out" or expect you to do something for them first, you have the wrong people helping you. People such as John Carew and John Lander get it. They offered to help and never asked for anything in return.

Remember Perry from the beginning of this chapter? He was the one who was able to make some connections for Susan and helped get her son accepted to Boston College. Susan's son was pretty sure he had the grades to get into Boston College. After the fact Susan told Perry that there were two other kids from this parochial school with slightly better grades and a higher class rank who did not get accepted to Boston College. Is that fair? Probably not, but that's life—just another reminder that it is not so much what you know, but who you know. Susan's son has learned this valuable life lesson at an early age. I am sure that if Perry ever needed a favor from Sue's family, they would do anything they could to help him. They will always remember what Perry did for them. That's another example of the power of *SuperNetworking* and what a strong network can do. Sometimes it is making someone's dream a reality.

Your Treasure Chest: Nourish It, Develop It, and Preserve It

I tell people all the time that my network of contacts is my treasure chest. Heidi, a successful sales executive, told me that her network of contacts is worth megabucks. Why? Because she invests in it every day. I found out that we had a lot in common. We both pride ourselves on having access to people and information, and we work on maintaining and expanding our network every day. It sounds so simple, yet it speaks volumes. Heidi exceeds quota every year and rarely if ever makes a cold call. She says she owes it all to the names she has in her Rolodex, which she has developed and nurtured over the years.

You must treat your network of contacts as you do any other thing you value. It is your lifeblood for future opportunities. Keep it fresh and up to date, and expand it. When you meet or speak to new people, whether you meet them in a business or social setting, on the plane, or anywhere else, immediately add their names to your database.

The reason people call me and ask for a favor is because they perceive me as a person who is well connected. They think I know everybody and stay in touch with everyone regularly. Of course I don't in fact know *everyone*, but if my ability to network makes them perceive me this way, it only serves to help me in the long term.

There are many ways to maintain the relationships or show your appreciation to your contacts and referrals. We covered some in Chapter 7. Here are a few more recommendations:

- ◆ Using the database fields, look at your list of contacts and put a check in the column that makes most sense as to how often you should be speaking with them. You can cross-reference this information with the date of last contact field. This will help you track your communication, ensuring that you are following up as planned, which will help you keep your network strong.

- ◆ Once you have implemented this process as part of your day-to-day routine, you will see immediate results. You will find that some people were more helpful than others, but everyone who you spoke with during the process must be thanked equally. Most importantly, be sure to offer your help to them.

- ◆ E-mail. Keep them short and sweet.

- ◆ For select people who go above and beyond, send a small gift to show your appreciation. This gift could be a book, golf balls, a picture, an ornament, or whatever you think makes sense. Although it's a small gesture, make sure you put some real thought into it. One year I went to the NCAA Final Four in Kansas City without tickets. My friend, Dave, was also out there as a guest of CBS Sports. While out there, Dave introduced me to his host, Hal. Hal mentioned he might be able to land me a ticket for the final game. One hour before tip-off Hal provided me a ticket in the ninth row, center court. The game was exciting. I had a great time and of course couldn't thank Hal enough. After the game I asked Dave how I could return the favor. He said Hal is just a genuinely good guy and was happy to help me out, and he thought it was not necessary. On my flight home I was thinking about what I could do for Hal. I thought back to the conversations I had with him over the weekend. I remembered him telling me that one of his favorite restaurants was Legal Seafood. When I got home I called Dave and got Hal's home address. I sent Hal and his family a clam bake package from Legal. To this day every time I see Hal and his wife they still talk about the great gift I gave them, yet I feel he did *way* more for me than I did for him. People who are critical to your success or help you out in any number of ways either personally or professionally must be recognized effectively.

◆ Personal updates really enhance these relationships. Let people know what's happening in your personal life (graduations, weddings, and so forth). This humanizes you and lets people see you in a different light.

Networking is just what Vince Lombardi, the legendary coach of the NFL's Green Bay Packers, said about winning: "It's not a sometimes thing, it's an all-the-time thing." That's the mindset you need to have in order to be successful at leveraging your relationships to sell more and make more money, as well as to be successful in life.

Invest in your network of contacts, nurture those relationships, develop additional referrals, and preserve what you have every day, and you will see immediate and long-term results and have greater fulfillment, both personally and professionally.

I See Your Future and It's...

You need to take a long look forward to understand that the *SuperNetwork* you build to sell more is the beginning of a lifelong process of *SuperNetworking*. In the future it will be your *SuperNetwork* that will provide the continuity, security, and many more options than people who do not have a *SuperNetwork* have.

Maintaining your *SuperNetwork* will be your golden parachute, providing you with financial security forever. A sales professional who is known to be successful and has a Rolodex worth millions will always be in demand.

By learning how to develop and maintain a lifetime business network, you will always be able to reach the person you need to reach. *SuperNetworking* provides the dynamic infrastructure for a productive and prosperous life.

You always hear people saying you must network, blah, blah, blah. They use the word, but few people going after new business have a plan such as yours. No other sales methodology shows people how to build on your own existing network of contacts and develop those into your *SuperNetwork*. You have been given a powerful, complete system that insures success. Go out there and make it happen!

Please help me share your networking success with others. You might want me to be a part of your network, and I might want to include you in mine. Reach out to me at *msalmon@salmonsays.com*.

Appendix

Here you'll find additional blank forms (as they appear in the text) that you can use. You may decide to modify or adjust elevator pitches, strategies, objectives, or scripts based on changes that occur, such as your profile of target accounts or territory, or find yourself in a different position. You can copy and fill in these forms as needed.

Elevator Pitch

_____

_____

_____

_____

_____

_____

_____

_____

_____

_____

_____

_____

_____

_____

_____

_____

_____

_____

Self-Analysis

Part I

(WRITE YOUR ANSWERS BELOW.)

What is my area of expertise?

_____

_____

_____

What has made me successful?

_____

_____

_____

What should people know about me personally?

_____

_____

_____

What should people know about me professionally?

_____

_____

_____

What distinguishes me from my competition?

_____

_____

_____

Part II

Now that you have a good idea about your field of knowledge, you must answer some questions about the benefits of doing business with you and your company.

What can a customer accomplish from working with me and my company? (features)

_____

_____

_____

What are the benefits of developing a relationship with my company and me?

_____

_____

_____

What should potential customers know about my service delivery? (tie in features and benefits)

_____

_____

_____

What differentiates my service from my competition?

_____

_____

_____

Why should a potential customer work with me and not my competition?

_____

_____

_____

How can I create or demonstrate the value my service delivers?

_____

_____

_____

♦ ♦ ♦

Planning Your Strategy

Evaluate your current position.

_____

_____

_____

Consider what to do differently to bring in more business.

_____

_____

_____

Determine what makes the most sense.

_____

_____

_____

Put the action plan together and execute.

_____

_____

_____

CONTACT LIST

"A" List	"B" List	"C" List	"D" List

Due Diligence

1. What does this company do and what industry is it in?

_____

_____

2. Based on all the research I have done, it appears that this company in which areas?

_____

_____

3. Based on what I know about the company and this individual, and my area of expertise, what is my value and my company's value to this company?

_____

_____

4. Who at this company would recognize and appreciate our/my value proposition to this organization?

_____

_____

5. What do I offer that is quantifiable, is measurable, and makes me and my product (or service) stand out from the crowd (both personally and professionally)?

_____

_____

Phone Script: Calling a Client or Contact

(Use additional sheets of paper as necessary)

Set the Stage.

_____

_____

Get Their Attention.

_____

_____

Value Their Time.

_____

_____

Set Expectations: Let Them Know What
You Are Looking For.

_____

_____

Trigger a Reaction and Generate an Activity.

_____

_____

Phone Script: Calling a Referral
(Use additional sheets of paper as necessary)

Grab Her Attention.

_____

_____

Value His Time.

_____

_____

Break the Tension.

_____

_____

Have a Definitive Positioning Statement.

_____

_____

Trigger a Reaction. (All calls should continue with "I could use your help.")

_____

_____

Index

About the Author

Michael Salmon is the founder and CEO of M. Salmon & Associates, one of the nation's foremost networking training and consulting firms. Salmon delivers seminars, workshops, and keynote speeches for major clients as diverse as Viacom, Merrill Lynch, UBS, New York Life, United Technologies, Capital One, Federated Investors, and Bank of America, to name a few, all of which make his *SuperNetworking* ideas a powerful part of their individuals' and organizations' future.

Salmon developed his *SuperNetworking* methodology over the course of his two decades of leadership in improving sales, marketing, and management processes for both publicly traded and privately held companies. Throughout his career he has been helping people find what they need by leveraging his network of contacts. Salmon is a PHD: Passionate, Hardworking, and Dedicated.

206 ◆ SuperNetworking for Sales Pros

Salmon is a recognized industry leader on the subjects of networking, sales, and career consulting. He is a much-sought-after speaker, explaining the power of *SuperNetworking*. He was a keynote speaker at Comdex 2003, between Bill Gates and Scott McNealy, and has been featured on television including FNC's *Fox & Friends*, CNN's *The Flipside*, Bloomberg TV's *Small Business*, NBC's *Weekend Today in New York*, and CBS's *Weekend Morning Show*. He is often quoted in national publications including *USA Today, Investor's Business Daily, L.A. Times, Chicago Tribune, New York News Day*, and *Entrepreneur* magazine.

His first book, *SuperNetworking: Reach The Right People, Build Your Career Network, and Land Your Dream Job—Now* was published by The Career Press and hit stores in November 2003.

Networking is a way of life for Michael Salmon. He has coached countless executives in his networking methodology and, as the remarks about his work indicate, he has changed the course of a great many lives. He resides in Framingham, Massachusetts.